for busy moms

HOW TO CLEAN YOUR HOME
fast

How to Clean Your Home Fast

Editor: **Vicki Christian**
Contributing Writer: **Michele Keith**
Associate Design Director: **Som Inthalangsy**
Copy Chief: **Terri Fredrickson**
Publishing Operations Manager: **Karen Schirm**
Senior Editor, Asset & Information Management: **Phillip Morgan**
Edit and Design Production Coordinator: **Mary Lee Gavin**
Editorial Assistant: **Kaye Chabot**
Book Production Managers: **Pam Kvitne, Marjorie J. Schenkelberg, Rick von Holdt, Mark Weaver**
Contributing Copy Editor: **Joyce Gemperlein**
Contributing Proofreaders: **Becky Danley, Juliet Jacobs, Mary Laughlin**
Contributing Indexer: **Stephanie Reymann**
Contributing Illustrator: **Chad Johnston, On Purpos**

Meredith® Books
Executive Director, Editorial: **Gregory H. Kayko**
Executive Director, Design: **Matt Strelecki**
Managing Editor: **Amy Tincher-Durik**
Executive Editor: **Benjamin W. Allen**
Senior Editor/Group Manager: **Vicki Leigh Ingham**
Senior Associate Design Director: **Ken Carlson**
Marketing Product Manager: **Brent Wiersma**

Publisher and Editor in Chief: **James D. Blume**
Editorial Director: **Linda Raglan Cunningham**
Executive Director, New Business Development: **Todd M. Davis**
Executive Director, Sales: **Ken Zagor**
Director, Operations: **George A. Susral**
Director, Production: **Douglas M. Johnston**
Director, Marketing: **Amy Nichols**
Business Director: **Jim Leonard**

Vice President and General Manager: **Douglas J. Guendel**

Meredith Publishing Group
President: **Jack Griffin**
Senior Vice President: **Karla Jeffries**

Meredith Corporation
Chairman of the Board: **William T. Kerr**
President and Chief Executive Officer: **Stephen M. Lacy**

In Memoriam: **E.T. Meredith III** (1933–2003)

All of us at Meredith® Books are dedicated to providing you with information and ideas to enhance your home. We welcome your comments and suggestions. Write to us at: Meredith Books, Home Decorating and Design Editorial Department, 1716 Locust St., Des Moines, IA 50309-3023.

Letter From the Editor

Dear Busy Mom,

You've sent out the S.O.S. and the smoke signals. You love to have your home tidy, clean, and welcoming. But it seems there's no time left in your hectic schedule to do this.

Between taking the kids to hockey, softball practice, choir rehearsals, parties, and other appointments, every day is full of chauffeur duties. Then add the mess, laundry, and clutter today's active families just naturally create.

Stir in cooking, dusting, vacuuming, and other everyday tasks. Throw in a pinch of seasonal chores, such as cleaning closets and washing the windows, and you've concocted a not-so-tasty recipe for stress. What's a mom to do?

Turn to the advice in this book. You'll find it easy, quick reading. From beat-the-clock ideas on how to save time on chores to how to create allergy-free kids' rooms, it gives you the lowdown on ways to establish a clean, safe place for your family.

From how to help prevent toddlers' messes to cleaning up pets' accidents, the tips are practical and helpful. You'll also discover fun ways to get your kids and your significant other, if you have one, to help clean without complaining. It's all here—everything you need to turn your place into a serene sanctuary.

Vicki Christian

Vicki Christian
Editor

Table of Contents

Chapter 1

Cut the Clutter

*"Housework can't **kill** you, but why take a chance?"*

—*Phyllis Diller, comedian*

Even when it's less than clean, a clutter-free house can easily pass the guest test. Why? Because visitors don't peek under the sofa or swipe a finger along the windowsill looking for dust. They simply get an impression, and "tidy" equals "clean." If you use these simple tips for tossing, organizing, and storing, you'll find yourself becoming clutter free and stress free too. In this chapter you'll find:

- How to organize to find things quickly
- Ways to repurpose items for storage
- Tips on maximizing shelf and closet space
- Solutions on what to throw, what to keep
- Decluttering techniques that add beauty to your home

Walk Right In

A welcoming entry hall sets the right tone—for you, your family, and everyone else who walks in the door. Rather than using it as a catch all where everyone in your family drops mail, boots, and hockey sticks, think of it as a real room. Then decorate and care for it with the same degree of attention you pay the rest of the house.

 Analyze your entry space first. What doesn't belong there? Where else could you put things?

 Start by clearing everything out of your entryway and seeing just how much space you have. Then consider what kinds of furniture and accessories will work best for you and your family's coming-and-going needs.

 Top a chest with a lamp, a vase of flowers, and a tray for keys. Designate drawers beneath for the kids' hats, scarves, and gloves.

Install a large, double-pronged peg for each child's coat and umbrella on one wall. Match the peg height to each child's height to encourage use.

 Lay the hallway floor with easy-care sisal or indoor-outdoor carpeting to avoid the kids tracking in rain, snow, and mud.

 Line up boots and other seasonal shoes under a bench. This provides seating while the bench hides them.

 Rotate closet contents with the seasons.

 Keep a stash of extra hangers in the closet for guests' coats. If there's no room, try a coat tree in a corner.

Use Living Room Logic

The living room is the place most families gather, where you usually entertain and that gets messiest fastest. It's easy to forget your sneakers there, and as for the kids and their toys? If you keep this one room in the house neat, you won't panic when friends or relatives show up unexpectedly.

 Stash magazines and newspapers in baskets. Toss them if you haven't read them in a week.

 Hide things under tables covered with floor-length cloths. Coordinate items with the rooms they're in—storage boxes in the basement, napkins in the dining room.

 Convert flea market finds, such as pretty suitcases in various sizes, into side tables and fill them with items you don't need every day. (It's low-cost decorating too.)

Utilize the space under stairways for bulky items such as tricycles and bowling balls.

 Decorate with multipurpose furniture such as trunks, ottomans, and window seats that open for storage.

 Train kids to remember that when they bring something into a room, they need to return it to its proper place.

BEAT THE CLOCK

I. **Put items** that can leave a mess, such as olive oil bottles, honey jars, and electric toothbrushes, on a tray or a sheet of aluminum foil before setting them on the shelf. If the bottles drip or the foil becomes dirty, you can replace it instead of scrubbing the shelf.

2. **Designate a laundry tub** or box for each child to stow his or her dirty clothes. When it's full, they can do their own laundry (with a little training from mom).

3. **Eat breakfast, lunch, and dinner** on trays and placemats for faster kiddie cleanup and longer-lasting tablecloths.

4. **Get everyone** to scrape, rinse, and place dirty tableware directly into the dishwasher.

5. **Throw sponges** in the dishwasher so there's always a clean one.

Declutter the Bedrooms

Create a retreat that helps you and your family begin and end the day in good spirits. Clear off bureau tops and put items where they belong—in the closet, drawer, or hamper. That way you don't have to face dirty socks and crumpled newspapers.

 Lose it if you don't use it. If clothes haven't been worn in a year but are still in good condition, pass them on to friends or donate them to charity.

 Hang necklaces, bracelets, earrings, and rings by category on T-pins arranged on a fabric-covered bulletin board. Choose a fabric that complements the room's colors.

 Store out-of-season clothes such as ski- and swimwear in appropriately marked boxes. Come vacation time, they're all together—ready for the suitcase.

 Create tablescapes by arranging perfumes, lotions, cufflinks, and watches on a silver tray on top of your dressing table or bureau.

 Use the space under cribs, beds, and sofas for extra storage. Store items in matching baskets if they're visible or plastic boxes if they're not.

 Put your kids' socks of the same color in see-through bags. This keeps drawers neater and makes dressing faster.

Memo from mom

JUST DO IT!

After moving to a larger house this past summer, I vowed to maintain order. But with three kids, three dogs, two cats, two horses, and a husband, that didn't happen. So I decided to simplify things by creating a master plan:

- Set a cleaning goal every day and stick to it, no matter how many times family members beg you to give it up.

- Clean a little bit every day—it only takes 21 days to develop a habit.

- Break down household duties into smaller pieces so they're easier to digest that way.

- Delegate age-appropriate chores to family members—they live there too!

- Find cleaning products that do the work for you, and not the other way around.

- Don't let housecleaning overwhelm you—and reward yourself for a job well done.

—from Carol Linnan, Indianola, Iowa
A busy mom to Meghan, 19 years old; Lane, 18 years old; and Quentin;
7 years old

Conquer the Closets

Opening a closet and having a hundred things fall out is only funny in the movies. A closet where everything is organized and accessible to kids makes every day better. Also, properly stored clothes and shoes keep their shape better and last longer, an important savings. Begin decluttering a closet by emptying it completely and getting rid of old or unwanted items. Remember, as you're yanking out all those mismatched gloves, cracked sunglasses, and unraveling scarves, some projects just need to look worse before they look better.

Tie jasmine sachets on hangers to keep closets smelling fresh.

 Make better use of shelves by placing items in baskets with handles, which are easier for kids to grab. This way they won't need to rearrange items on the shelves.

 Fit closets with double-hung rods for half-length items or place a bureau underneath for foldable ones.

 Find children's shoes easily by keeping them in the original boxes identified with the style, color, or photo.

 Organize clothes by type, then color. Clean, repair, or discard them before storing them for the season.

 Attach hooks to closet door interiors or use over-the-door organizers for belts, bags, and hats. (Make sure the smallest child in your family can reach the items.)

Create a Spalike Bath

Even with kids, a tranquil, spalike bathroom is possible. Give each family member a brightly colored bucket for favorite bath items—soap, yellow duckies, shampoo, or nail brushes. Keep them under the sink or line them up on the bath ledge. The buckets will add a fun note to the room and help create order.

DID YOU KNOW?

In 1886, American Josephine Cochran proclaimed, "If nobody else is going to invent an automatic dishwashing machine, I'll do it myself." And she did.

Check the expiration dates of items in your medicine cabinet periodically. Toss them out when their time is up, even if the container isn't empty.

 Roll towels and store them in an urn or oversize flower pot. You'll always be prepared for guests, and there'll be more room in the linen closet.

 Let kids have fun consolidating the leftover contents of shampoo bottles while bathing in the tub. Ditch the empties.

 Gather bathroom cleaning supplies into a big beach pail under the sink. It's a great way to make cleaning day and in-between touch-ups a breeze. Just make sure the space is not accessible to tiny ones.

 Conquer container-itis. Keep just one shampoo, conditioner, and soap in the shower or tub at a time. As they're used, replace them.

 Keep personal care items out of sight. If the counter is the only place available for makeup, arrange it in a variety of nonbreakable containers in splashy colors.

Organize It Easily

Think of yourself as the CEO of Home, Inc. As with any business, your aim is maximum efficiency with the least amount of effort made by a happy workforce. Anything that saves space, time, or steps is the way to go. Just like at an office, everything needed on a continual basis in your home should be within arm's reach.

Separate serving dishes by use: everyday, entertaining, barware, and special occasion. Design a portion of storage space to each use. Label shelves. If you need a storage unit, visit your local home improvement store.

 Try curtained shelves in the dining room to store your kids' books and toys if you're using the area as a study space.

 Construct banquette seating for two sides of your breakfast nook or dining area. It's a terrific look and adds extra storage space if the bench lifts up or the sides slide open. If you're not so handy, have it done professionally.

 Hang narrow shelves inside the cupboard doors for spices, cereal, and other packages.

 Create a closet for the ironing board. Open and the board comes down; close the door and it folds up and away.

 Attach a notepad and pencil to the pantry door. Jot down supplies as needed for an ever-ready, up-to-date shopping list.

 Keep measuring spoons in frequently used items, such as coffee, flour, and sugar.

DID YOU KNOW?

During the early 1900s in England, housemaids employed at elite estates were kept busy during their regular 16-hour days. They tackled a never-ending list of chores, including washing floors, lighting fires, laundering sheets, and emptying the chamber pots of each member of the family.

Design a Handy Office

Whether it's a den or a corner of the bedroom, a home office needs to be efficiently organized to keep family or business matters running smoothly. Your family's health and financial well-being can be dependent upon such documents as vaccinations, surgeries, and major home repairs. It's worth an hour a week to file them so you can find them quickly.

 Store supplies in hanging shoe organizers. Attached inside a door, supplies stay out of sight yet easy to access.

 Clip useful articles in magazines and newspapers; put them into the appropriate file immediately. (It's best to make folders for subjects such as home cleaning tips, decorating ideas, and information on appliances.) Then recycle them and throw older publications out.

 Attach wheels to file cabinets and slipcover them to match the room décor. This way they're easy to roll into place when and where they're needed.

 Divide file cabinets into those dealing with family issues, and those with business. Within each cabinet, make sub-divisions for family members, real estate records, and such.

 Create low-cost, extra-deep shelving with a country look by attaching sturdy fruit crates to wall studs with screws.

Clear Those "Other" Rooms

The good news is that most people have attics, basements, laundry rooms, and garages. The bad news is that most people have attics, basements, laundry rooms, and garages. It's human nature to toss "stuff" there. Here's how to keep these rooms clutter-free, too.

Throw it out or give it away if no one wants, needs, or uses the item. (This could be a great way to get rid of your life partner's neon blue bowling trophy from high school.)

 Don't buy large quantities of something just because it's on sale if you've no room to store it.

 Categorize and keep items together, then clearly mark storage containers, such as holiday decorations, out-of-season clothing, or hobby supplies.

 Hang as much on the walls as possible—chairs, bikes, garden hoses, and lawn mowers. It frees floor space in a fun way.

 Hide stuff in containers, under skirted tables, on shelves, and behind curtains, screens, and doors. Mark the containers clearly so you can find the items later.

 Consider custom cabinetry. It's a wonderful way to get cupboards and closets into even the most oddly shaped spots.

CALL IN THE PROS

If decluttering seems overwhelming (in other words, sends you to bed with the covers over your head), think about hiring a professional organizer. Consider contacting the National Association of Professional Organizers at 847-375-4746 and hq@napo.net. They'll review your situation, prepare a plan to meet your specific needs, and get you going in the right direction.

Chapter 2

Choose Your Method

"To thine own self be true."

—*William Shakespeare, playwright*

House Chores

dust rooms ✓
vacuum ✓
scrub floors ✓
shake rugs ✓
take out trash
bathroom

Everyone is different, with various likes and dislikes. And that's as true for doing housekeeping as it is with creating fashion and food. Since cleaning just has to get done, the least we can do is make it as efficient as possible.

So choose the system that works best for you, regardless of what your best friend, life partner, or neighbors might say. While cleaning may not ever make it to your 10 Favorite Things to Do List, it will go faster and be easier.

Consider:
- When your energy level is the highest
- If weekends or weekdays are best for cleaning
- Whether attacking a project all at once or bit by bit works best for you
- If you can do everything yourself or if you need help
- Whether certain rooms or areas need more work than others
- What you can do in the future to make all this housekeeping less time consuming

Which of These Works Best for You?

There's no right answer here, but thinking through the various approaches below and deciding which one best suits your personality will help you keep on top of the household cleaning chores.

- **Top to Bottom and All the Way Around**
  In each room, start at the door and inch your way around, beginning at the top and working your way down (remember, dust falls). First dust, then wash or polish, and finally vacuum.

- **One Room or Floor at a Time**
  Even small homes and apartments can be overwhelming. Try attacking one room or one floor each week.

- **Ten Minutes Daily**
  Many chores can get done in 10 minutes when we set our minds to it. Fridges can be cleared and wiped down; laundry can be folded and put away; sheets can be changed; sinks and toilets can be scrubbed!

- **Bring in the Troops**
  Whatever it takes—bribery, games, threats, rewards, or a family powwow—get together your significant other (if you have one) and the children who are old enough to help, then divide up the housework chores. (Who says you have to do it all by yourself?)

- **Is Silence Golden?**
  Do you like the serenity of no extra sounds—or do you play rock and roll, blues, and classical music as you clean? Whatever satisfies and motivates you is the answer here.

Set a Schedule

Figure out what needs to be done every day, weekly, monthly, yearly, or seasonally. It's easy to get sidetracked, but by sticking to the schedule, you'll get everything done in a timely fashion. This way you won't repeat a task until it's necessary. For example:

Daily

Declutter
Sweep the kitchen floor
Wipe the bath and kitchen countertops
Make the beds
Load/unload the dishwasher

Weekly

Dust
Vacuum
Clean the toilet
Change the sheets
Change the bath/kitchen towels

Remove the litter bag from the car (if you don't have one, now's the time to get one unless you're planning on the litter elf doing it)

Sponge off plant leaves and water indoor plants

Monthly

Dust and clean vertical blinds

Wash and sanitize garbage cans

Fluff up bed pillows with a run through the dryer

Verify that fireplace glass doors open and close securely for safety

Spot-check the medicine cabinet and fridge for outdated items and toss those

Check the washing machine and the dryer for gum, ink, or other stain-causing buildups

Seasonally/Yearly

Wash the windows or hire someone to do it

Hire a chimney sweep to clean and check the fireplace

Have carpets and sofas professionally cleaned

Inspect the basement and attic for pest infestation, cracks, or leaks

Review and organize important family documents and files

Check your family's clothes for items that might be outgrown or worn out and give them away.

Check Out the Outside

You already have so much to think about inside the house, but don't forget to keep the outside of your home and the surrounding area safe as well as looking good. You should check:

- **Screen doors and windows** for rips, tears, or rust, and repair them promptly so you don't attract burglars.

- **Birdfeeders** to see if they're working well.

- **Inground and aboveground pools** for cracks. If you find them, repair them or have them professionally repaired.

BEAT THE CLOCK

1. Make a to-do list for hired help. Keep them on track and ensure your satisfaction.

2. Use a little bleach to get stains out of coffee mugs and pots and pans fast. Just be sure to rinse the items thoroughly.

3. Attach special-care instructions on hangers of garments needing special treatment. That way you won't forget and throw them in with the kids' soccer uniforms.

4. Fold and smooth cotton items immediately after drying to eliminate ironing (unless you find ironing therapeutic).

- **Sidewalks, paths, and driveways.** Cracks or areas with missing concrete are unsightly and unsafe. Have them professionally repaired.
- **Shrubbery and trees.** If some are dying, remove them and consider replacing them. Keep the tag on the plant or tree showing the date you bought it and the greenhouse where you purchased it. Many greenhouses will replace the item for free if you've negotiated that up front.
- **Porch and balcony railings.** If these are rickety, you and your kids could fall. You could also face a lawsuit if guests or service people trip.

Declutter First

Don't even try to clean around piles of newspapers and toys on the living room rug. If things get put away regularly, there shouldn't be much prep work needed come cleaning day. Pick up first and then begin cleaning. *(See Chapter 1 for tips on decluttering.)*

Try Four Big Boxes

At least twice yearly, do major decluttering using the 4-Box Method. Most useful for clothes, it works equally well for everything else. Unless you're incredibly brave, get the OK before attacking anyone else's closet or the garage. You don't want to donate Sis's favorite jeans or the drills others in your family use.

 Start with a room a week or every two weeks, depending on your schedule and patience, until the entire house is finished.

 Begin by labeling four large boxes "Keep," "Donate," "Dump," and "Fix."

 Keep clothes that make you look and feel great, are in good condition, and that suit your lifestyle and needs.

 Donate any items you've outgrown (when you lose those five pounds, you can buy some new ones) or are out of style but that someone else might enjoy wearing.

 Dump any clothes so bad that no one would want them—stained, ripped, or otherwise damaged items.

 Schedule a time to review the clothes and other items you've decided to keep to decide what to do with them.

 Place items you're saving, but need some repairs, in a bag or box. Separate them into categories such as:
- Needs dry cleaning
- Needs professional tailoring
- Needs repairs you can do yourself

TIP 58 **Donate anything** that, for whatever reason, you love but haven't worn or used in one year. If you want to save it for sentimental reasons, store it in a safe, dry place.

 TIP 59 **Do all of these steps** the same day if you can to completely finish the project. Then mark it off your list—it's soooo satisfying.

Exit Strategies

Many organizations would be thrilled to accept your donations of cast-off clothes, household items, decorative accessories, and kitchen equipment. Call first for pickup and delivery times and options.

 TIP 60 **Bring items** to a consignment shop. If they're accepted and sold, you usually reap 40 to 60 percent of the selling price.

 TIP 61 **Give them to a church,** synagogue, or mosque. Besides giving items to their own congregations, religious institutions frequently collect for disaster relief efforts.

 TIP 62 **Donate to the** Salvation Army, Goodwill, or homeless or battered women's shelters. These organizations have large trucks, making them the perfect recipient for entire dining room sets, bedroom suites, and large single pieces.

DID YOU KNOW?

A 2004 U.S. Department of Labor study found that, "...the average American woman spends one hour and 20 minutes on household chores every day."
Girls, it's not getting less, so now's the time to get organized.

Hold a garage or yard sale. It's a fun way to make new friends and turn trash into treasure.

 Be realistic. If you want to have a garage sale, be sure you realistically have the time to:
- **Organize** items
- **Label** each item with a price
- **Clean and set up** a space to hold the sale
- **Arrange the items** logically and attractively
- **Advertise the event** in neighborhood shoppers, grocery stores, and with garage sale signs at both ends of the block where you live
- **Get rid** of items that didn't sell

 Help kids learn math and business skills by involving them in garage sales. Kids love to help price items, take the money from buyers, or sell food and drinks for a reasonable cost (and maybe get a little spending money of their own).

 Set up a booth at a flea market. Newcomers are often needed to fill empty spaces.

 Visit an auction house or antiques store. These establishments often have walk-in appraisal days and will take an item if they think it will sell. You'll have to negotiate the price with them.

 Consider selling items on the internet. Millionaires are made by selling some of the weirdest stuff (vintage pink poodle lamps, someone's soul, dust bunnies in the shape of Delaware, potato chips that look like Elvis—you get the idea here).

HOW TO HIRE A PROFESSIONAL CLEANER

- **Ask friends** for recommendations.

- **Compare rates** and plans; find out if there are extra costs for particular tasks such as washing dishes or doing laundry.

- **Check references** and/or your Better Business Bureau.

- **Get legal questions** answered. For instance, are the workers bonded or insured? Are you liable for worker's compensation if they're hurt on the job?

- **Try responsible teens** if you're restricted on your budget. With just a little bit of instruction from you, they may do a good job—and you'll save money. For example, professional services charge $60 to $90 to clean a two-bedroom, 860-square-foot-house. You could hire a teen you know for $20 to $30 for the same work.

- **Be home** the first few times to give instructions, verify that you have all the equipment they need, and confirm that you approve their work.

Be Creative with Containers

Tight for space? Not a problem. Incorporate storage as part of your decorating scheme whenever possible. Stash items inside cupboards and closets as well as out in plain sight.

 Search flea markets as well as catalogs for étagères, those freestanding shelving units that come to us via France. In so many wonderful styles, colors, and materials, there's one right for every room.

Line up flat baskets on the bedroom bookcase to hold papers; old hat boxes for odd-shaped or larger items; or small one-of-a-kind plates to hold jewelry, hair clips, and rubber bands.

 Don't hide pretty pitchers in the kitchen cupboard. Free up that space and use the pitchers for pens and pencils on your desk, makeup brushes in the bathroom, cooking utensils on the counter, or crayons on the kids' homework table.

 Put plastic or wire dividers into drawers to separate cutlery, jewelry, or makeup. Line the dividers with an antitarnish cloth if you're storing silver.

 Hang tracks under shelves for wine glasses.

 Install cup hooks for cups and mugs.

 Attach a counter-to-ceiling grid to the kitchen wall. Use S-hooks to hang cookware and utensils. Or use a smaller grid to show off your copper pot collection and add color to the room.

 Ask "What else could this hold?" when you buy storage bins.

Save Your Documents and Save the Day

Even in this computer age, there are many documents that need to be kept in hard-copy format. Anything that relates to a family member's health, finances, or real estate falls into this category. The documents to save are listed on the following page.

Your kids' inoculation and vaccination records needed by schools.

 Wills and organ donor statements.

 Bills for repairs made to the home inside and out that could affect its price and value when it's time to sell.

 Receipts for decorative home additions that would stay if you sell your home. These could include tiles, lighting fixtures, wall-to-wall carpeting, and fireplace mantels.

 Schedules of medical checkups for each family member, especially if there is a specific problem that requires special tests or frequent visits to the doctor.

 Insurance forms, referrals, and payments.

 Any tax-related information and back tax returns for at least eight years.

DID YOU KNOW?

WARNING: *Lazy folks, perhaps some even in your own family, who don't like house cleaning may:*

- *Use the dog as a mop.*
- *Tie sponges on the kids' shoes and dip them in soapy water so they can "skate" the floor clean.*
- *Dry the kids and themselves with towels still damp from the last time.*
- *Use paper towels when the toilet paper runs out rather than going to the store to buy more.*

Manage Your Time

Just as with a big corporation, running a house means managing time wisely—yours and everyone else's. Here are a few successful strategies:

 Time your chores—dusting, vacuuming, polishing the silver. Then try to beat your last times.

 Stay on task no matter how tempting that phone call or TV show might be.

 Use every moment. Fold the laundry while the chicken is roasting. Sort magazines if you're put on hold. Fix a hem during TV commercials. Empty the dishwasher while the coffee's brewing. But schedule a half day weekly for R & R.

 Simplify cleaning methods by taking preventive action. It takes less time and effort to scrub a pot that's soaked overnight. Sinks and tubs sparkle if they're wiped out after every use. Drains stay clearer longer if hair is removed when it's still in the sink, not down the drain.

 Help stop clogs from forming by pouring a commercial solution for this purpose down your drains monthly.

Just Do It

Do it now so you don't have to do it later—unless you prefer to stay inside cleaning while everyone else is enjoying the beach or the first high school football home game of the fall season. Doing things such as the tasks on the next page during extra time is the best way to go:

Pick up anything that's in the wrong place and put it where it belongs—in the drawer, closet, or on the hook—so you can find items when you need them.

 Inventory supplies such as toilet paper, canned goods, and cleaning products. Using a magnetized list on the refrigerator works well. Replace the items before they're completely gone.

 Mop up spills before they turn into impossible-to-remove stains.

 Toss something if it needs to be tossed; fix it if it needs to be fixed. Don't just hang on to items endlessly without a plan of action.

Going Pro

So what's your pleasure? Some gals would rather skip vacation than do housework. Do you need only an occasional break or help when the baby arrives? If you can afford it, hire a professional home cleaner as required:

 Yearly as a special treat. For goodness' sake you deserve it! Sit back and tell someone else what to do for a change.

 Monthly for the dirtiest, most difficult, or least favorite rooms to clean—perhaps the kitchen, bath, or garage.

 Bimonthly because you've recently redecorated and want to clean and protect your beautiful new digs.

 Weekly because you can now afford it with your new job.

 Twice a week because you haven't gotten a good night's sleep since the baby was born.

Keep Them Safe

Now that you have cleaning tasks under control and your home is spotless (at least maybe on one good day a month), keep it safe from pollutants and other items that can put you and your kids at risk.

 Have gas appliances professionally checked for leaks.

 Say "no" to smoking, even to guests. It causes eye, nose, and throat irritation, not to mention cancer. And it's a bad example for your kids.

 Look out for lead, especially in homes built prior to 1970. If you fear your child has ingested lead, get a simple blood test by a pediatrician to determine risk and possible treatment.

 Test for radon with kits available from hardware stores and home centers. Contact the American Lung Association at 212-315-8700 for details.

 Keep prescriptions, over-the-counter medicines, laundry supplies, and any other potentially damaging items out of your kids' and pets' reach. Tightly seal these containers.

DID YOU KNOW?

About 40 percent of home accidents are slips and falls. To avoid these:

- Keep floors clear and uncluttered of kids' items—from toys to clothes.
- Make sure all rugs adhere well to the floor (rubber-backed rugs are the best).
- Never let anyone climb onto counters to reach something.

Reward Yourself

The housekeeping comedy queen, Erma Bombeck, said, "My theory on housework: If the item doesn't multiply, smell, catch fire, or block the refrigerator door, let it be." Kidding aside, do treat yourself for all your hard work.

 Close the bedroom door and take a well-deserved snooze.

 Treat yourself to premium ice cream, such as candy jar chocolate or white chocolate with raspberry and chocolate. Don't even look at the calories or fat grams on the carton.

 Send the kids to Grandma's, get dolled up, and join your best pals for a girls' gab lunch.

 Ask your partner, if you have one, for a romantic evening, just the two of you.

 Give yourself a spa treatment, complete with a facial, manicure, and pedicure, all at a leisurely pace.

 Indulge in a trial size of a new perfume or wild nail polish such as *POW Pink* or *Passion in Purple*.

 Save your change every day in a special box, vase, or bank. When it's full, turn it in for cash at the bank and take yourself to lunch.

Chapter 3

Recruit Your Kids to Help

"If you want children to keep their feet on the ground, put some responsibility on their shoulders."

—Abigail Van Buren, author of Dear Abby newspaper advice column

You wouldn't part with your kids for all the money in the world, but oh, can they be annoying! From the sticky fingers wiped on the walls and the bathtub ring left for someone else to sponge off to the mud tracked on the carpet, sometimes it's just too much. Train them from day one by turning cleanup into a game and you can, and will, survive. Read on to learn some easy tips and secrets that work.

- "Monkey see, monkey do" applies here. Set a good example for your kids by hanging up your clothes, cleaning spills immediately, and returning things to their rightful place right away.
- Ease children into doing chores as they grow. Start with simple ones like having them pick up their own toys.
- Visit the kids' schools, even day care, to pick up good ideas for keeping rooms neat and tidy.
- "Music soothes the savage beast," it's been said. Play music as you clean—your kids' favorites—and kids might surprise you with some help.
- Turn cleaning into a bonding experience for all.

Go for Games

When it comes to getting your kids (and sometimes your life partner) to help keep the house presentable, using a game works. Small children can't see behind the deception. While the older ones can, acting just like kids might be what they want. Try any of the following tips for every age of child (including that grown-up person hiding behind the newspaper):

TIP 110 **Turn Mom's little helpers** into speedy cleaners by using an egg timer to clock each chore as a game. Put each child's score up on a chart. Reward the kids with the fastest times stars or a special one-on-one activity with Mom or another family member.

Show your kids how to make the ring around the bathtub go away with the "magic" sponge that's been layered with soap.

 Pretend the toy box is a basketball net and the toys are balls. Give points for each toy that gets into the box. Keep a tally that your child tries to beat each week.

 Exchange your kids' toys with those of the neighbors every so often. This way they're always new and exciting, and you'll save money too.

 Organize chores such as dusting, vacuuming, and picking up dirty clothes into one-step tasks your kids can do on consecutive days. Give gold stars for success.

 Play musical dusting. Rev up the boom box with one of your child's favorite tunes. Play it loudly as you and the other kids dust. Then stop the music. Put on the next kid's favorite songster and dust again.

 Have your kids wear old socks on their hands and dust walls and large spaces that are free of delicate objects.

Play Hide and Seek

Storage can be a problem, especially if you don't throw or give away those things you no longer need or use. So get creative with your storage solutions. Ask your kids for advice too. Their perspective might produce some fabulous ideas for you.

Put paintbrushes and other messy art supplies into outgrown rubber rain boots for easy cleanup. Put a rock in the toe to keep them upright or nail one side of the boot to the wall itself. Have your children organize playthings into several large containers. They should use a different color for each category—art supplies, games, dolls, blocks, etc.

 Cover the bedside table with a floor-length cloth. Voila! You have extra storage space.

 Have Junior put his or her PJs inside the pillowcase. This creates a neater bed, and your kids will always be able to find their pajamas.

 Use window seats as extra storage space. What a great place to put out-of-season clothes or holiday decorations.

 Equip kids' rooms with foldable canvas director's chairs. They're great when friends come over and are easily stored flat under the bed. Let your kids choose the colors.

 Install bookcases with movable shelves to make storing things such as footballs and basketballs, trophies, and baseball bats easy. It also creates instant wall art. Get your kids involved by allowing them to choose the items to display.

 Be creative. Anything that's big enough can act as a storage unit, such as a stack of vintage suitcases, old-fashioned hatboxes, oversize pails, and plant urns. Let your kids help choose them and they'll be more likely to want to pick up after themselves.

BEAT THE CLOCK

1. Avoid bathtub rings by avoiding oily bath preparations. Use a water softener if you live in a hard-water area.

2. Initiate a no-food-no-drink policy in children's bedrooms. This reduces the number of crusty plates under the bed or glasses with milky residue hidden in the closet. Less intensive cleanup for you!

3. Put a doormat made of a rough material such as straw inside kids' bedroom doors and have them wipe their shoes on it before entering. It saves you frequent mopping or vacuuming.

4. Plan your routine and stick to it. Children thrive on order and will be more likely to help if they know exactly what's expected.

5. Clean mirrors monthly, not daily, to keep them shiny and bright.

Closets

Besides being great places to throw things and shut the door, closets are also wonders of organization. When you and your kids have arranged them properly with everything at your fingertips, you'll all feel good.

 Use hangers for more than just clothes, especially when kids are small. Toddlers' cups, babies' teething rings—even teddy bears—can be neatly hung on them.

 Affix rods and hooks inside closet doors to hang belts, bags, caps, and jewelry. Let your kids arrange them.

Repurpose bookcases that are too small for your book collection as shoe racks for the kids' closets.

 Use kids' caps and hats as wall decorations if you're short on closet space. They'll love helping you place them in a circle or line them up along the furniture rail.

 Apply car wax to a sticking door to ease opening and closing. Kids will think this is cool.

 Keep a lightweight vacuum cleaner or electric broom in the kids' closets. They can use it to keep their closets free of dust bunnies between major cleanings, with just a little bit of quick instruction from Mom.

Doin' Dressers

Categorize items in the drawers so they can be found easily and quickly. Rather than piles, which are difficult to keep neat, use dividers such as the ones made for silverware. Designate different drawers with a picture handdrawn by the child to help him or her remember where things go.

 Tighten the loose screws on dresser knobs by removing the stripped screw on the knob, covering the stripped area with clear fingernail polish, and replacing it. Let your kids apply the polish.

 Tell your teens that returning dirty clothes to drawers is a good way to attract bugs.

Prevent moths from laying eggs in woolens by storing items in zippered plastic bags and placing them in drawers.

 Use emptied aftershave bottles to keep your sons' drawers and the items in them smelling nice. They may prefer soap bars still in their wrappers.

Bubble, Bubble, Toil and...

It's hard enough to get some kids to brush their teeth and take a bath, let alone help keep the bathroom clean. But by showing them fun, easy ways to do it, you might get more help.

 Let children pick the color for their bath towels. You'll know if they're being used, and there'll be less arguing about whose is whose. And they'll have lots of fun shopping for them.

 Show tweens how their favorite grooming product—hairspray—can remove buildup on mirrors by spraying it on and wiping the mirrors clear with newspapers.

 Delegate age-appropriate bathroom chores. Even little ones can fold towels. Older kids can empty the trash.

DID YOU KNOW?

William Blackstone built the first clothes washer with a boxlike tub and hinged lid. Powered by the operator, it appeared in 1874. Before this, happy homemakers hauled water into a huge kettle, built a fire, and boiled clothes in steaming soapy water. More fun—they used a long stick to stir clothes and pull them out. We've come a long way, baby!

Ask your kids to take the throw rugs in your home outside and wallop them (the rugs, not the kids). They'll vent their frustrations and have fun, not to mention get the dirt out of the rugs too.

 Use club soda or seltzer water to clean chrome. Kids will probably enjoy this task because of the fizz.

 Schedule a big-time bathroom cleaning right after someone has taken a steamy bath or shower. The dirt will have loosened, making your job easier and faster.

 Rev up the kids with a bath cleaning game. Write bathroom chores on small pieces of paper and have each kid draw one. They'll love gloating over the kid who drew scrubbing the toilet.

Laundry Lore

Short of living in a nudist colony, there's not much one can do but attack the laundry frequently. Get the kids into helping you early on in life.

 Simplify laundry for young children. Ask them to help wash, dry, fold, and put away a load each day. By doing it regularly, you won't have a mountain of laundry come the weekend.

 Teach preschoolers to match socks and hang up things by color.

 Let children put on mittens and wash as though they were washing their hands. Presto—clean mittens and fun too.

TIP 144 **Make folding laundry** a game to see who can make their stack the highest without the pile tipping over.

 TIP 145 **Teach a great** laundry lesson. Take one white and one bright red worn-out T-shirt. Have your kids throw them in the wash in super hot water. They'll be grossed out when the white one turns a dingy pink.

 TIP 146 **Create a colorful** "Let's Do Laundry" chart with your kids, letting them choose the colors. List all laundry chores and use fun stickers to show when the task is done—and by whom. For an especially well-done job, attach an extra smiley sticker.

Memo from mom

CORRAL THOSE DOLLS

Here's a great anticlutter strategy my daughter and I came up with for toys and other stuff. Together we chose easy-to-access bins to put under her bed for:

- Her own dress-up clothes
- Fashion dolls
- Fashion dolls' clothes and accessories (even the shoes tuck into a small box inside the accessory box)
- Her own bathing suits

When she's done playing, either with a friend or alone, she just tosses everything into the right box and kicks it under the bed.

Basically, my view that works is: If the storage plan isn't easy to execute... fuggedaboutit. Works great for us!

—from Suzanne Sokolov, Auburndale, New York
A busy mom to Dana, 8⅓ years old, and Zachary, 12½ years old

Chapter 4

Quick Kiddie Cleanup

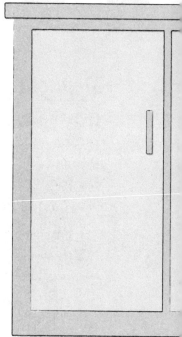

"Oh, no!
Not on the silk sheets!
Not on the silk sheets!"
—Film character Jack Holden,
Three Men and a Baby

You're not alone in thinking that all babies and toddlers do is eat, sleep, and create messes for you to clean up. It's true, at least for a while. The good news is that there are lots of ways to make life easier until they outgrow this phase. A few helpful things to keep in mind:

- Be a mother, not a martyr. If you need help, get it.
- Stay positive. Even if you detest housework, fake like you enjoy it so your kids will develop a positive attitude about it. Who knows? You may fake yourself into a better attitude along the way.
- If your child can grow up thinking decluttering is a game, both of you will benefit.
- When you must choose between a clean room and time with the kids, choose the kids every time. You'll never be sorry.

Ease the Eating

While children are learning how to drink and eat properly, and, of course, when they're babies, food will be dropped. It will land not only on the table, but on you, themselves, and the floor. With foresight and planning, you can enjoy every meal no matter how messy it gets.

 Cover the floor and a few feet beyond the high chair with an oil cloth or rubber matting that's easy to clean and will fold and store quickly.

 Do the same thing under your child's chair when he or she starts eating at the table.

 Use plastic or easy-care fabric placemats or trays with a generous lip if food is more often off the plate than on.

 Speed up learning with cutlery scaled to fit tiny hands and fingers.

Protect yourself with a full-size smock and baby with a bib. Have plenty on hand so you can at least start off clean.

 Promptly rinse dishes used for egg and milk dishes with cold water and then wash.

 If you make baby's food yourself with a pressure cooker, wash it after each use, but don't immerse the cover. Instead, wipe with a sudsy cloth, rinse with a damp one, wash the gasket, and clean the opening with a pipe cleaner.

Solve Sleepy Time Blues

Preschoolers have a sense of ownership and a developing need for privacy. Encourage this while you help them to fall asleep quickly by providing bed linens and pajamas in their favorite colors. Here are some more tips:

 Change and launder sheets and pillowcases weekly to get rid of dust mites that feed on human skin.

 Wash blankets and mattress pads monthly or as needed.

 Avoid using chlorine bleach on flame-resistant fabrics, especially kids' pajamas. It reduces the chemicals' effectiveness and can ruin treated fabrics.

 Test intercoms as well as smoke and carbon monoxide alarms monthly. Replace batteries as part of your regular housekeeping routine.

 Give baby's room a delicious smell in the winter by putting several drops of essential oil or perfume on the heat registers.

Eliminate dust mites from bedding by putting bedcovers and sheets in a garbage bag and tying tightly. Put the bag in the freezer for an hour to kill the nasty little critters.

 Wash foam pillows in the washing machine and air dry rather than using the dryer. They'll retain their shape better.

 Check labels of duvets for cleaning instructions. Some can be washed and dried in your machines; others must be dry cleaned.

Baby ABCs

A major part of your life with a baby will be protecting it, caring for it, and cleaning up after it. Here are tips:

 Before baby comes home, set your thermostat on your water heater to 120 degrees F or less for safety. Or buy an antiscalding device, available at most home stores.

 Never leave your baby unattended in the bath. If the phone rings or someone knocks at the door, wrap your baby in a towel and bring him or her with you.

 Place a bucket of mild detergent and hot water next to the primary changing table each morning. Let baby's dirty items soak before putting them into the washing machine.

 Keep a baby bag packed with all the necessities so you can pick up and go at a moment's notice. Try to remember to replenish as needed.

Reserve a corner on each floor of the house with everything needed for changing...unless you're training for the marathon and really love climbing stairs.

 Use dye- and fragrance-free detergents for washing cloth diapers to protect baby's tender skin.

Clean Toys and Surfaces Often

Clean toys, bottles, and eating utensils often. Check labels for directions and keep in mind that anything with a sound box or mechanical parts can't be put into the washing machine or dryer.

 Place stuffed animals in a paper bag with baking soda to clean them. Shake the bag well. Remove the toys from the bag and shake each animal to rid it of excess soda.

 Check for torn seams and loose buttons before throwing stuffed animals and dolls into the machine. Repair before washing.

 After your child has played outside, remove his or her shoes or clean the bottom of them. Socks help to keep floors and furniture clean, and occasionally not wearing shoes can aid in the foot's healthy development.

 Store crayons and other small toys in the divided plastic organizers intended for silverware.

 Keep big tin gift containers filled with popcorn or cookies after they're empty. They make great toddler seating as is or covered with a fabric to match the room's décor.

 Clean laminate table and bureau tops with a paste of lemon juice and baking soda. Finish by rubbing to a shine with a soft cloth.

Declutter Babies' and Toddlers' Rooms

The sheer amount of "stuff" in babies' and toddlers' rooms can make keeping them tidy a challenge. By putting toys, books, and clothes away every day, rooms will look clean even if they really aren't. Here are some hints to help you get ahead in the decluttering game.

 Spot check furniture cushions for small toys, buttons, and coins before you vacuum because these items can block and damage the vacuum hose.

 Keep separate laundry baskets for colors, whites, and delicates in the closet or built into the cupboard of your baby's room.

 Consider a trundle bed for toddlers. The extra bed beneath can be used for storage until they're old enough for sleepover guests.

 If space is limited, use a plastic garbage can as a bedside table and fill it with out-of-season clothes, gear, or toys your child has outgrown. Securely attach wood to the top, add a floor-length tablecloth, and put glass over the cloth to create a handy nightstand.

 Encourage kids to read while keeping their room neat with a pocketed bedskirt where they keep their books.

 Keep baby's ointment, bottle, talcum powder, and other similar items handy and together in a wall hanging made with pockets. Purchase or make one out of terrycloth so it's easily washable, and hang it above the changing table.

Be a Washing Wizard

Sticky fingers are a big part of growing up. And as one would expect, small children often use curtains, bedspreads, sheets, and upholstery as their own personal napkins. So unless you're willing to laminate everything in your kid's room, follow these easy guidelines to keep it sweet smelling and germfree:

 Foam cushions are comfy for kids but fall apart if they become too wet. When cleaning, don't soak.

 Be proactive to save time and effort. Make sure fabrics for kids' rooms are silicone treated. If not, spray silicone on the fabrics yourself to prevent dirt buildup and stains.

 In between washes remove dust and dirt from drapes and curtains by vacuuming. Use the upholstery attachments because brush attachments can damage the fabric.

 Take large drapes to a self-service laundry that has larger capacity machines or have them professionally cleaned and treated.

 Remove hooks or weights from drapes before washing them so the fabric won't be damaged.

 Wash lined drapes following the washing instructions for the weakest fiber listed in the blend of fabric.

DID YOU KNOW?

As a Peace Corps volunteer, Ann Moore saw mothers in the African country of Togo carry babies on their backs. So she and her mother designed a similar system for Moore's first child. Their baby carrying device was patented in 1969.

BEAT THE CLOCK

1. **Don't put baby's clean clothes** on for the day until you've fed her. It's a great way to avoid accidents that could soil clean outfits.

2. **Layer the crib** with several sheets and waterproof pads for faster changes.

3. **Record baby's immunization** shots on a paper calendar or in a special file in the computer so you always have an up-to-date record. This way you won't have to waste time rummaging around for these items before doctors' visits (especially important for emergency trips).

4. **Store extra sets** of crib sheets in baby's room. When washday arrives, you'll have a clean set at hand.

Keep Lace Lovely

They're so sweet and ever so popular—lace bed linens and curtains for nurseries, lace-trimmed socks and bonnets for newborns, and little lace pinafores and accessories for toddlers. Yes, lace is delicate and needs a bit of extra care, but with the right techniques, you can keep it bright and white.

 Soak items made of and trimmed with lace in warm, sudsy water to clean them. Then rinse. Don't rub, twist, or wring; just swish gently in the water and lay flat to dry.

 Try whitening nylon lace curtains with a commercial product made for whitening lingerie, available at home stores. Rinse well after using the product as directed.

Brighten lace pieces by first soaking them in cold water before you wash them.

 Hang lacy curtains and garments over the laundry line while still slightly damp. Creases and wrinkles will smooth out naturally and save you ironing time.

Cleaning Walls and Ceilings

Paint flies off the brush, gum sticks in the weirdest places, crayon strays from the paper and onto the walls. What's a mother to do? First, remember: This too shall pass. Then on cleaning day, or while the kids are napping, attack with fervor.

 Clean washable wall coverings with an all-purpose cleaner. Be sure to rinse thoroughly to avoid leaving a film on the wallpaper.

 Wipe down nursery room murals with a clean, damp sponge only if they're made of heavy-duty poster paper. Use soft brushing movements because scrubbing hard can cause surface damage. Call the manufacturer to determine the mural's composition if you're unsure how to clean it.

 Spray decorative moldings with a general cleaning solution. Use a paintbrush or old toothbrush to remove dirt in the crevices. Then spray the area with plain water and dry with a soft terry cloth towel.

Clean glass over framed baptismal certificates, photos, and other precious art with a soft cloth sprayed with rubbing alcohol.

Dust the ceiling with the dusting attachment fitted to your vacuum hose, a long-handled feather duster, or a flexible broom head. You can also tie an old diaper over the head of a broom.

 Wash off fingerprints and other marks immediately. Never scrub plaster or drywall that hasn't been sealed or painted.

Bright Ideas for Lamps

Bulbs and shades are dust magnets. Keep them clean to provide stronger light. Wipe unplugged cords off with a sponge dampened with warm soapy water or commercial cleaner. Here are more tips:

 Begin cleaning a lamp by removing the shade. Dust or vacuum the shade and then wipe the bulb with a dry cloth.

 Wash glass or plastic globes and reflectors in warm, sudsy water. Rinse and dry carefully.

 Clean glass bases with a damp cloth wrung out in clear or sudsy water. Clean porcelain, glazed stoneware, and china bases with a cloth wrung out in mild sudsy water. Rinse and wipe dry with a paper towel or lint-free cloth.

 Use a feather duster on metal or paper shades.

DID YOU KNOW?

Research shows that women today do two-thirds of the household chores. Men would have to increase their contribution to keeping things neat and clean by 60 percent to achieve a level equal to that of women.

Vacuum lampshades lightly once a year to remove dust. Don't plunge them into water unless you know that treatment to be safe for the shade.

Hit the Floor

If the floor is clean, you won't panic when baby begins to crawl. Be it wall-to-wall carpeting, area rugs, linoleum, or hardwood, floors are prime targets for the worst kind of dirt—that which comes in via shoes. Begin by barring outdoor shoes from kids' rooms if at all possible.

 Damp-mop painted floors with a mild detergent solution using as little water as possible.

 Clean hardwood floors by damp-mopping a small area with warm water. Then immediately wipe the surface dry.

 Wash glossy enameled floors with hot water to cut through the dirt.

 Wash waterproof varnished floors with warm soapy water.

 Remove stains from rugs and carpeting as soon as possible so they don't set.

 Scrape up solid spills on rugs and carpeting with the back of a knife. Don't rub. If the spill still shows, apply carpet stain remover. For the toughest stains, call in the pros—the sooner the better.

 Remove marks on linoleum by rubbing gently with medium-grade steel wool dipped in turpentine or paint thinner. Then wash the area with sudsy water and dry.

Memo from mom

SOLUTIONS FROM A STEPMOM

Living as a couple is one thing, but marrying someone with a child and turning into a stepmom overnight—like I did—is another.

If you're new to motherhood with toddlers, tiny hands mean sticky surfaces. Here are my tips:

- With small kids come small hands and smudges. Clean glass tables and windows with newspapers to keep them from streaking. It's a great way to recycle.

- Paint the walls of nurseries and toddlers' rooms with semigloss or gloss paints for a nice and easily washable surface. Then you can use any type of green cleaning solution to clean fingerprints and handprints from walls.

- Use a small amount of cooking oil to remove sticky residue on hard surfaces. Just put the oil on a paper towel and rub the surface until the residue disappears.

Samantha, Atlanta, Georgia, a busy stepmom

Protect the Floors

The flooring for babies' and toddlers' rooms is costly, both in original price and the amount of time you spend caring for it. Do yourself a favor and protect it. The more you shield it from wear and tear, the longer it will last.

 Use sturdy plastic rounds to securely cup furniture legs and protect your floor from scratches. Really heavy furniture requires soft, textured rounds to protect the floor.

 Install self-adhesive rounds for lightweight furniture. Replace them when they're worn.

 Look for plastic squares in dark and light tones to blend with wood floors. They can usually be found at hardware stores and home centers.

Use screw-in protectors for furniture you move often. Choose smooth ones that won't harm hard-surface floors.

 Protect carpets from compression dents with rounds and squares. Look for clear acrylic ones that blend with any color or pattern.

 Place doormats on the interior of your home as well as at the front door, by steps leading from the basement, and in front of the garage. They trap dirt so it's not tracked in to the little ones' rooms.

Use Sweet Scents

Small children smell so sweet when they're clean from the bath. Funny how fast that delightful fragrance disappears. At least you can keep tiny ones' drawers, closets, clothes, and linens smelling fresh. Just read on:

 Take everything out of children's dresser drawers yearly, vacuum them, and then wipe them down with a damp rag and fresh-smelling cleaner.

 Put a sachet in each drawer. Oranges covered with cloves or sprigs of lavender collected in a cloth bag are two easy ones you can make (and save money too).

Rid new wood furniture of that dry smell by placing an opened box of baking soda in each drawer for a few days. Then replace the boxes of soda with dryer sheets. Fill the drawers with clothes.

 Be sure clothes are thoroughly dry before putting them in closets, cupboards, and drawers. This will prevent mold and mildew from forming.

Mop up musty smells in noncarpeted closets with a solution of 1 gallon warm water, $\frac{1}{2}$ cup vinegar, and $\frac{1}{4}$ cup baking soda. (Don't use this on hardwood floors.)

 Put a dryer sheet in toddlers' sneakers at the end of the day. They'll smell fresh as a daisy come the next morning.

 Tie scented dryer sheets to a few hangers in the closet. The scent will freshen closets without being overpowering.

Decorate the Childproof Way

Decorating is more than just making things pretty. Well-planned designs and thoughtful product choices can actually reduce the amount of time you spend cleaning babies' and toddlers' rooms. Finishes, types of paints, and placement of furniture are among the things you should consider.

 Semigloss paint works best for children's rooms, playrooms, and baths because it's scrubbable, durable, and less likely to show marks. If you prefer a flat finish, choose a light color, which is less likely to show fingerprints.

 Add a top coat of water-base polyurethane over paint projects in babies' and kids' rooms for easy cleanup.

 Choose a desk that can be raised and lowered. Give your toddler a pint-size chair and let him or her use the desk for art projects. Switch to a full-size chair and raise the desk when your child is ready to spread out textbooks instead of crayons.

Use plates, trays, and old paintings as inexpensive, colorful ways to decorate nursery walls. When your child is older, mix in some larger artwork and posters that reflect his or her interests and hobbies.

 Pass up cutesy, juvenile shelving. Instead, buy simple units that you can paint different colors and decorate in various ways as your child grows. You'll stretch your budget too.

 Be realistic. Children are bound to leave toys out. Select a living room coffee table with cubbies or open shelving in its base or place a large, decorative urn or basket in the corner of the dining room for fast, last-minute pickup.

 Use artificial rather than real plants to add greenery and life to any child's room. Placed on top of armoires or other high places, no one will know they're not real. This way you won't have to worry about watering them or your baby or toddler tipping them over and getting injured in the process.

 Involve your kids in decorating their rooms when they're about 5 years old. If they have a say in the theme, colors, and bedspread, they have a tendency to take more pride in their rooms and keep them neater.

Chapter 5

Blast Through the Bath and Kitchen

"A woman is like a tea bag. You never know how strong she is until you get her into hot water."

—Eleanor Roosevelt, former First Lady and humanitarian

Baths and kitchens are not only seen and used by friends and family more often than other rooms of the house, they're important to everyone's physical well-being. No matter what it takes, it's important to keep them clean and germ free to lessen the chances of getting sick from bacteria and viruses.

- Invisible germs are as much your target as visible dirt. It's an ongoing battle to be rid of them. Use disinfectants to make them disappear for the moment, but be ready for their return tomorrow.
- Slick surfaces, electrical appliances, and pointy objects can turn kitchens and baths into dangerous places, especially for little ones. Be sure to unplug appliances before washing and to keep them away from water-filled sinks and tubs.
- Put locks on low-level cupboards holding medicine and cleaning supplies if you have small children or nosy pets. These cleaning agents can be deadly if ingested.
- Use the dishwasher to clean anything that fits into it—such as toys, knickknacks, or file holders. If you have doubts as to durability, let the items air dry because the dry cycle is the harshest.

Create an Easy-to-Clean Bath

With a few accessories such as matching towels, pretty soap, lighting fixtures with dimmers, TVs, mirrors, and piped-in music, your bath can have a luxurious, spalike feel. If you take a bit of time to declutter every day, cleaning won't take long.

 Keep the bath romance-ready by collecting toys and other kid stuff in a plastic bucket under the sink or in a cupboard.

Hang pictures on slick bathroom surfaces such as tile and marble with suction-cup hooks.

 Add delicate fragrance with scented candles for a beautiful, spalike feel.

 Put bathroom cleaning products in a pretty, covered container if you're space challenged. They'll be there when you need them, but won't ruin the relaxing ambience.

 Save wear and tear on the floor with attractive bathroom rugs. They're so easy to throw in the wash when they get dirty. Pick ones to coordinate with your color scheme just as they do at elegant spas. Make sure they don't skid—ones with rubberized backs work well.

 Add a few drops of essential oils in lemon, lavender, pine, or mint for a pleasant smell when you clean with vinegar. It's great for dissolving hard-water stains.

Create serenity with leafy plants. Plus, being in a moist environment means you barely have to care for them. Stick them under the shower once in a while for a good watering.

Use Kid-Friendly Ideas

When they're small they run around too much; when they're big they stay holed up in their rooms. With a few fun ideas, you can make sure tiny tots don't get into trouble and older ones lend a hand when you need it. Read on to see what might work for you.

Install hooks attached to suction cups for hanging robes, washcloths, and back brushes. They're easy to move as kids grow and their needs change, and they're available in a variety of sizes.

 Choose white tubs, toilets, and sinks. They cost less than those in colors and are actually easier to clean.

 Check out the new and affordable heated towel bars and cupboards. Kids will take baths more willingly when you dry them with a warm towel.

 Keep bath mats sparkling with whitewall tire cleaner. Apply the cleaner to the mat outside and let it soak a few minutes. Then scrub and rinse off.

 Induce older children to shower by letting them choose their own shower curtain. Make sure it's plastic so you can wash it on the machine's delicate cycle and then hang it up on the shower rack to dry.

 Stop mildew that can form along the bottom of shower curtains by cutting off the portion with the mold.

 Teach older kids to clean the toilet by letting them pour a can of cola into the toilet bowl first. If they let the cola sit for an hour, scrubbing away stains will be fast and easy.

 Suggest that teens help clean bathroom mirrors with shaving cream. It keeps the mirrors fog free, and it's kind of fun too.

Memo from mom

LET SMALL THINGS GO

In a general sense, learning when to let small things go, and prioritizing what really needs to be cleaned, goes a long way toward keeping one's sanity. Here are some of my tips:

- To save time in the morning, I prepare lunch bags the night before.

- I also get the clothes the kids will wear the next day ready the night before. Those 15 minutes before bedtime save a lot of time in the a.m.

- To help keep things tidy, I stow small toys in the colorful plastic boxes from baby wipes. They're stackable and store well in cabinets or on shelves.

- To make cleaning less burdensome, I delegate to Dad weekly cleaning chores that require some serious elbow grease.

—Michèle Gates-Moresi, Chevy Chase, Maryland
A busy mom to Jo, 8 years old, and Lili, 14 months old

Quick Cleaning

Sometimes it's just too much. Everything gets dirty at the same time, and it's usually when somebody's boss or relative stops by for an unexpected visit. With planning, you can avoid a large number of housecleaning problems, and be prepared for a sneak cleanup even while the doorbell is ringing.

TIP 244 **Grab cotton-tipped swabs** from the medicine cabinet to clean the crevices in light switchplates and around the faucets. (This might be a good job for the kid who let the dog chew bubble gum.)

TIP 245 **Put bathtub stoppers** along with scrubbing sponges in the silverware basket of the dishwasher. They'll come out germ free, as well as clean.

Let your kids put denture-cleaning tablets in the toilet overnight for a sparkling bowl.

 Keep a paper towel on the microwave's revolving dish to speed up cleaning.

 Run the dishwasher through its entire cycle with a cup of white vinegar once a month to reduce soap scum.

 Keep a spray bottle with a solution of I part of bleach to 4 parts of water or an all-purpose spray cleaner for quick cleanups.

 Use products such as sprays and gels for small areas and powder or liquid cleaners mixed in a pail of water for larger ones.

Take Care of Tiles

The array of bathroom tiles these days is mind-boggling. From iridescent squares with the look of the sea to handpainted ones with folk designs to tumbled marble that echoes Pompeii, there's something for every taste. Follow these hints to keep the grout holding them together equally beautiful.

 Scrub grout with a mild bleach solution or use a bleach pen. Don't use abrasive pads.

 Use a penetrating, commercial grout sealer to help prevent future stains.

Whiten stained grout with a strong bleach solution (¾ cup bleach to I gallon water) and scrub gently with a small brush.

Clean grimy grout around the tub area with an old toothbrush dipped in full-strength vinegar or liquid disinfectant.

 Try rubbing alcohol or a chlorine mixture (¼ cup bleach to 1 gallon of water) for cleaning caulking around bathtubs.

 Apply foaming bath cleanser and let it work for a few seconds. Then whisk away residue with a brush or sponge. Rinse and wipe dry.

 Squeegee bathtub and shower tiles to keep them shiny and free of soap scum after the last shower of the day.

Clean With Noncleaning Products

So you've been holed up and haven't been to the store in weeks? That doesn't really work as an excuse. You probably still have everything you need right in your kitchen. Besides getting the cleaning done, you'll save money too.

 Pour 1 cup of baking soda down the toilet bowl weekly to avoid clogging and odors.

 Wash and shine fixtures and mirrors with rubbing alcohol and a soft cloth.

DID YOU KNOW?
When you really feel like screaming, cursed with too much to do and too little help, remember that in manor houses of Edwardian England, the lower-ranked maids' daily duties included emptying and cleaning the family members' chamber pots with a vinegar-soaked rag kept for this purpose.

Use baking soda on a damp cloth for a nonabrasive cleaner for the porcelain fixtures.

 Detach decals by heating them with a hair dryer while you pry them up with a plastic spatula.

 Use coffee filters and glass spray (or vinegar and water) for clean, lint-free mirrors.

 Remove fly specks from painted window frames with cold tea or use a soft cloth dipped in a mixture of equal parts skim milk and cold water. A rough cloth works better than a smooth one.

Store It Smart

No matter how big your house, there never seem to be enough places to store stuff. And once the kids come along, forget it! The answer to the problem is to use your imagination.

 Build shelves, or have them professionally built, to hold towels. They'll be out of the way yet within handy reach and will stay clean until they're needed.

 Replace a small, mirror-front medicine cabinet with one that spans the width of the counter. It will hold more and look much nicer.

 Take advantage of unused air space by installing chrome poles that can be fitted with towel racks and shelves.

 Take stock of the stuff you have stashed before even thinking about new storage space. Maybe some of it is old, empty, or otherwise useless. If so, toss it and free up new space.

BEAT THE CLOCK

1. **Clean** the razor with your nail brush after each use in the shower.

2. **Put** the cutting board in the dishwasher along with the dishes.

3. **Load** the dishwasher back to front and put silverware into baskets by category—knives with knives, spoons with spoons, and so on. This will save you precious minutes looking for a free spot when it's full, as well as saving time when you put things away.

4. **Dab** a bit of perfume on the tops of lightbulbs for a pleasant aroma.

5. **Leave** the shower doors open after you've showered to allow the air to circulate and dry surfaces.

 Try all-purpose cleansers rather than having a different cleaner for each function. You can also borrow from the kitchen, using dishwashing liquid to clean floors, for example.

 Consider that vanity sinks look more welcoming when there are pretty things on top. Rather than storing makeup brushes and pencils in the cabinet, store them in delicate vases on top.

TIP 270 **Make the most** of the space you do have. Put shampoos, conditioners, and shaving creams in wall niches, or in caddies that hang over the showerhead pipe.

 Store overflow items in a chest of drawers in the hall outside the bathroom door.

Now That You Know...

What you should do in the bathroom, and soon will know how to handle the kitchen, it's smart to know what you should not do in these two labor-intensive rooms of the house. So unless you want a daily headache, major stress, or wrinkles and gray hair before your time:

- Don't clean up any family member's mess if he or she is old enough to do it.
- Don't go on a search-and-destroy mission for dust bunnies daily.
- Don't give in to your quest for perfection by arranging the items in the medicine cabinet by size and color.
- Don't invite guests over at the last moment if your children have been lounging about the house all day. Some surprises aren't pleasant.
- Don't try to save money by buying cheap toilet paper.
- Don't economize by using flimsy aluminum foil as plastic wrap.
- Don't economize by gathering slivers of soap and melting them into one of normal size.

Enjoy a Comfy, Clean Kitchen

Open-style kitchens are all the rage and can look fabulous. But having one means cleanliness is more important than ever. While dinner is cooking or you're waiting for the toast to pop up, do little things such as sponging spills off cupboards and appliances or wiping out the fridge's veggie bin and re-lining it with a paper towel.

 Sterilize a dry sponge by putting it in the microwave for 30 seconds at full power. A wet sponge needs a full minute.

 Save the sink and cut cleaning time by keeping a rubber grid on the bottom of the sink.

Use paper towels to wipe up meat juices and blood rather than a sponge or cloth. Throw the towels in the garbage, spray the area with disinfectant, and wipe it dry.

 Grind lemon or lime slices through the garbage disposal every few days for a fresh smell.

 Clean the blender and food processor by squirting a few drops of liquid soap into them. Fill halfway with warm water, cover, and whip away. Rinse and repeat if necessary.

 Dispose of up to 200 pounds of grease a year with a fan above the stove. Clean the filter regularly.

One Germ Is One Germ Too Many

Bacteria and germs love food and beverages as much as we do. The kitchen is their target because it gives them a playground of places to live, grow, and breed. Killing germs in garbage cans, on countertops, and elsewhere will keep your kitchen spotless and your family healthier. Here is some advice for eliminating them.

 Encourage everyone to wash their hands often and for a good 30 seconds with soap and hot water.

 Use antibacterial solutions to wash hands often when cooking and cleaning.

 Buy garbage cans with tight-fitting lids to keep flies out, especially during the hot months when they and mosquitoes are out in full force.

 Use disinfectant on all surfaces in the kitchen. Do this prior to cooking and as you clean up.

Store food in containers that act as barriers to pests. Plastic, glass, and metal containers with lids that fit tightly will keep food safe.

 Caulk around doors and windows where ants might come in.

 Choose waffle-weave cotton cloths as your top kitchen-cleaning tools. Use one to wipe off dirty surfaces and another for dishes. Try different colors for each task to keep them separate.

TIP 285 **Use two** chopping boards, one for vegetables and the other for raw meat. Because germs can live for several hours, scrub the boards in hot soapy water, rinse in hot water, and air dry immediately after use.

Protect to Prevent

They used to say, "Make hay while the sun shines." Today's version for busy Moms is, "Do it today so you don't have to do it tomorrow." A few minutes of prep time can save hours and stress, as well as money down the road.

 Apply a coat of paste wax on chrome, plastic, fiberglass, and marble surfaces to repel dirt and hard-water deposits.

TIP 287 **Damp-mop** vinyl floors with a mild detergent solution. Polish them with a water-base latex polish and seal them with a water-base sealant.

Don't use solvent-base cleaners. Dirt on vinyl tiles can become ingrained in the cracks. Don't use wax polish, paraffin, or turpentine on rubber flooring for the same reason.

 Avoid scrubbing dirty windows with a dry cloth; it will scratch the glass.

 Season skillets and fry pans as manufacturers dictate. This will keep them working better longer.

 Organize placement of appliances, cooking tools, and cleaning equipment so that things you use most frequently are up front, and the others are in the back.

 Defrost the refrigerator regularly and keep ice cube trays filled. This will keep it operating more efficiently.

 Put place mats under dog and cat food dishes. Dump spills into the garbage. Then toss the place mats in the dishwasher.

DID YOU KNOW?

The first self-cleaning house was developed by Frances Gabe after World War II. She lives in her prototype in Oregon, where each room is outfitted with a "cleaning/drying/heating/cooling" device. A powerful jet of soapy water is sprayed throughout the room, which is then rinsed and blow-dried. It also has self-cleaning sinks, bathtubs, and toilets. While Gabe holds 68 patents, the house has not yet come to life for the rest of us.

AT LEAST YOU DON'T HAVE TO MAKE YOUR OWN SOAP!

If you're facing a dirty bathroom and piles of crusty dishes in the sink, it could be worse. Much worse. You could have lived in the pioneer days and have had to make your own soap from lard and lye, quite a time-consuming process. You'll be glad you don't have to do this:

1. **Collect ashes** from the fireplace or burn tree stumps and gather those ashes.

2. **Put the ashes** in a barrel or hollowed-out log.

3. **Add water to the ashes.** (Lye is formed when the ashes soak in water.)

4. **Get out** the huge black kettle and put the lye, lard, and water into it.

5. **Boil this** over a fire you make outside. After a few hours the mixture thickens and you pour it into a pan to harden.

6. **Cut up** the hardened soap into squares or bars. (All the way along you had to be careful: The lye could burn skin, and it was unhealthy to breathe the fumes.)

Fab Floors

With everyone hanging out in the kitchen, a clean and shiny floor is important. It's not so tough if done on a regular basis, and spills mopped up sooner rather than later won't be as likely to cause problems.

TIP 294 **Add a cup of** vinegar to a pail of mop water. It cleans dirt and grime and gives floors a shine.

 TIP 295 **Pour salt on** a fresh liquid spill and let it set for an hour. Vacuum or blot the salt with a paper towel and change towels as they become saturated.

 TIP 296 **Flip the mat** you have in front of the sink around periodically. This way, all areas will wear evenly and soiling will be evenly distributed.

 TIP 297 **Keep wood floors** from being too slippery—don't use wax with a hard-seal finish.

Clean Safely

Reaching for high spots on ladders and wiping up water and spills add up to danger when cleaning the kitchen. Take time to prepare for safety's sake. Follow these simple tips:

 TIP 298 **Wear comfortable old clothes** that aren't so baggy that they'll catch on a ladder or prevent you from seeing the rungs and buckets underneath.

 TIP 299 **Cover your wrists** with sweatbands to catch drops of scrub water and keep your hands dry.

 TIP 300 **Make sure** the stepladder is square on the ground and opened all the way before stepping on it.

 TIP 301 **Wear rubber-soled** shoes for climbing ladders or standing on countertops.

 TIP 302 **Don't use water** near electrical wall sockets and lights. You could get an electric shock.

 Disconnect electrical appliances before you begin cleaning.

 Don't leave the bucket at the foot of the ladder where you or your children could step into it. Move the bucket before moving the ladder.

 Spread newspapers on the floor to alleviate hazardous puddles of water.

Winning Windows

Sparkling clean windows indicate a well-kept home. While you might want a pro to do it after winter's onslaught of dirt-filled snow and rain, the rest of the year you'll need to maintain them, unless the window fairy keeps them crystal clean.

 Tackle window cleaning on an overcast day to avoid smears. The sunshine causes unsightly streaks, causing you extra work.

 Recycle used tea leaves to make a terrific window and windowpane cleaner. Add them to a little water and wipe down surfaces with a soft, lint-free cloth.

 Clean large areas of glass with a squeegee instead of a cloth. Start at the top and work down, frequently wiping the blade on the cloth to limit streaking.

 Use vertical strokes to wash your windows on one side, and horizontal ones on the other. That way you'll know on which side of the glass streaks remain.

Pick a chamois cloth, lint-free dishcloths, or newspapers and paper towels for cleaning windows. All work well.

 Remove dried-on paint with a flat, razor-type scraper or safety blade. Always work in one direction. Don't scrape backward and forward, because you may scratch the glass.

Keep Bugs at Bay

City, 'burbs, or country, bugs abound, especially in hot climates. Carrying disease, bugs can appear in even the cleanest homes. Keep your house bug free for healthier, happier living.

 Cover food and dirty dishes tightly if they must be left out. Flies' eggs hatch in 24 hours and can spread disease-causing bacteria quickly.

 Stuff steel scrubbing pads into any gaps between pipes and walls. Bugs and rodents can't get through these.

 Get rid of cobwebs when they're new. Once covered with grease and dust, they're more difficult to remove.

 Wrap cheesecloth around the end of a yardstick, secure it with a rubber band, and spritz it with a cleaning-dusting spray to remove high cobwebs.

 Discard old fruit and vegetables. As they are, they'll attract fruit flies and cause the still-fresh ones next to them to spoil also.

 Don't leave food out, uncovered, in the kitchen. Make sure dirty dishes aren't piled in the sink. Buy garbage cans with tight-fitting lids to keep insects from enjoying a feast.

Kill ants with a mixture of 1 part borax with 1 part powdered sugar. Scatter it over a piece of stone or wood near the nest's entrance.

 Replace sponges frequently. Odor means contamination.

Watch Cooking and Storing Times

Safe food storage includes holding foods at a proper temperature while serving them, cooking them to a desired temperature, cooling hot foods quickly, and storing leftovers. Here are a few tips:

 Keep foods colder than 40°F or warmer than 140°F, even on your holiday table. The danger zone for food temperature is between 41°F and 140°F.

 Cook poultry, stuffing, and stuffed meats to 165°F; ground meat to 155°F; injected meats to 155°F; pork, beef, veal, and lamb to 145°F; fish and fresh shell eggs to 145°F; and any potentially hazardous food cooked in the microwave to 165°F for at least 2 minutes. In doubt about the age of a leftover? Toss it to be on the safe side.

 Cool hot foods quickly to prevent bacterial growth. Do as famous chefs do and put hot soups, stews, and gravies in a container in an ice bath and stir them now and then. The more quickly they get into the fridge, the better.

 Store leftover food in tightly wrapped plastic or in plastic containers with tight-fitting lids to avoid leaks. Attach a label to the container with the name of the food and the date. Use the "first in, first out" method that chefs use so leftovers won't stay in the refrigerator too long and spoil.

Get Rid of Roaches

More frightening to many than a lion in the house, roaches haven't changed in 300 million years. They still like to hang out with humans. Luckily, it just takes five easy steps to get rid of them:

- **Keep your home dry.** Roaches need water daily to survive. Fix leaky faucets, clean up dampness with towels, and don't leave water in sinks or tubs.

- **Use drain stoppers** for all baths and sinks.

- **Clean kitchen surfaces,** such as countertops and shelves. Roaches are attracted to areas where other roaches have been so get rid of their "trail."

- **Stir together** equal amounts of baking soda and powdered sugar. Leave the mixture in a shallow bowl where you have seen roaches. This mixture is poisonous to them.

- **Call an exterminator** if pests persist to get advice about how often a visit is warranted and what the costs might be.

DID YOU KNOW?

Archaeologists tell us there's evidence of indoor plumbing in palaces dating back to 2500 B.C. But it took an enterprising American, New Yorker Joseph C. Gayetty. to invent the toilet paper to accompany this new-fangled gadget. He came up with the invention in 1857, calling it "The Therapeutic Paper" because it contained aloe. Sold in packs of 500 sheets for 50 cents, it had the inventor's name printed on each sheet.

- Forty percent of the world's population lacks indoor plumbing.
- A low-flush toilet can save you 18,000 gallons of water a year.

Chapter 6

Dash Through Living Areas

"I hate housework. You make the beds, you wash the dishes, and six months later you have to start all over again."

—Joan Rivers, comedian

With everyone in the family going in so many directions at once and you trying to carve out a little time for yourself, you may want to close your eyes and pretend the mess isn't there. But when you know the tricks below, it's much simpler to keep main living areas and bedrooms clean.

- Take five minutes to pick up main living areas before hitting the sack each night so the next day begins clutter free.
- Create the illusion of clean with made beds, an uncluttered coffee table, and a fireplace mantle adorned with candles rather than soda cans and CDs.
- Bust those dust bunnies behind furniture and under radiators. They can cause sinus problems and allergies because they're dust mites' favorite places to hide.
- Tame technology. Circle the spaghetti like messes of wires into doughnut shapes, secure with twist ties, and tuck out of sight. It will make the area look less cluttered and be safer too, because kids won't trip on the wires.

Bedrooms

It would be so easy to simply shut the door, but could you live with yourself? Of course you could.

Children spend one-third of their lives in bed—babies even more. Purchasing, caring for, and maintaining their beds and the linens you put on them is important not only for a comfortable night's sleep but also for their physical well-being.

 Bring the outdoors into bedrooms by airing pillows and comforters outside. It's even better if you can dry the sheets outside too.

TIP 325 **Flip and rotate** mattresses so the surface remains flat. Strong teens are great for this task.

 TIP 326 **Vacuum mattresses** on both sides each time you flip them to rid them of any persistent dust mites.

 TIP 327 **Find excellent storage** space in an old-fashioned trunk placed at the foot of the bed.

 TIP 328 **Don't use** aerosol furniture polish on antique beds. Although it gives an instant shine, it doesn't fill the scratches as well as wax.

 TIP 329 **Before polishing** old wood beds, check for cracks or lifting. Don't use wax if there are any damaged areas. It can make gluing loose pieces back difficult.

 TIP 330 **Get a special dry cleaning bag** or laundry hamper for every family member's closet, including each of your kids' closets. Have them dump dirty clothes into it as they take clothes off. Let them choose the type of bag or hamper they want in their favorite color.

 TIP 331 **Wax or polish** painted floors to make them easier to clean.

 TIP 332 **Keep bedroom bureaus** and tabletops clutter free for speedy dusting. Get pretty baskets to put magazines and newspapers in.

 TIP 333 **Teach your children** a neat trick: Smooth sticky drawer runners with a quick rub of a white candle or sprinkling of talcum powder.

Floors and Walls

Surround yourself with wall coverings and flooring that give you and your children a sense of serenity. It will be more pleasant to keep these tidy this way.

 Shake, then dust draperies using a vacuum cleaner.

 Scrub floors with a mixture of mild disinfectant and warm water. This way you won't mind so much if toddlers drop their sandwiches on the floor and then eat them.

 Vacuum fringed rugs with the nap of the rug. Be cautious that the vacuum cleaner brush does not become entangled with the fringe.

 Take advantage of wall space by building shelves. Intersperse books and plants for a homey look.

 Use a dry mop for cleaning hardwood floors. This prevents moisture from leaking between boards in the floor.

 Try dry newspapers, not paper towels, to clean wet windows and prevent streaking.

 Avoid smoking inside if you want your paint job to last longer. Over time, smoking will cause a gray film to form.

 Show your kids how to make and apply nail-hole filler. Just mix 3 parts baking soda and 1 part white household glue. As it dries, it tends to shrink, so you might have to add a bit of water before painting. Kids usually enjoy putting this filler in holes.

 TIP 342 **Never use** ammonia products to clean mirrors. When the silver backing along the edge reacts with the ammonia, it may turn black.

Furniture Delights

If you can combine practical with pretty when selecting furniture, especially with kids in the house, you'll be way ahead of the game. Look for surfaces that are easy to clean, offer extra storage space, and are a size and height convenient to the kids.

 TIP 343 **Wipe lamp bases** of unglazed ceramic with a damp cloth and glazed ones with lukewarm water and a mild detergent. Dry them thoroughly for best results.

 TIP 344 **Dust furniture,** even painted pieces, with a cloth spritzed with lemon-scented dusting spray. It does the job and makes the entire room smell good.

 TIP 345 **Place clocks** on level surfaces such as bureau tops, away from direct sunlight and heat vents. Clean them using the same method you would for furniture made from the same material.

DID YOU KNOW?

Crazy-making cleaning tasks should be skipped. Just say "NO" to:
- *Using toothpicks to get to the hidden grime in the holes on the telephone receiver. (Some grime can remain hidden forever.)*
- *Arranging all your canned goods alphabetically, in the exact order of expiration dates.*

TIP 346 | **Remove** sticky residue on antiques with a cloth dampened with white vinegar. Gently rub the area, then polish it with a soft cloth.

 TIP 347 | **Don't consider** suede furniture if you have kids under 18 at home. Spills can be difficult and expensive to treat.

BEAT THE CLOCK

1. Use toys such as wagons, pup tents, and doll carriages to store stuff quickly in kids' rooms.

2. Protect electronics such as computers, stereos, and DVDs with plastic covers when not in use to avoid the need to dust.

3. Use flip-top hassocks that double as containers for extra seating and speedy decluttering.

4. Dust windowpanes and sills with the vacuum's brush attachment rather than a cloth. It's so much faster.

From the Inside Out

The simplest things in life can make anyone smile. Tops among them have to be beautifully organized closets and drawers that smell as good as they look. It doesn't take much to achieve this, but it does require daily maintenance. But oh, it's so worth it!

Help your kids make a hamper out of large boxes for each of their bedroom closets. Poke a few holes in them for ventilation. This way you won't faint when you remove your kids' soccer or basketball clothes.

 Store a window cleaner, grease cutter, and dusting spray in each bedroom closet for ever-ready access.

 Banish musty odors by rubbing the inside of drawers with oil of wintergreen.

 Discourage moths in closets with sachets of dried lavender or cedar bark. Don't let cedar chips touch clothes; they can turn clothes yellow.

 Wrap keepsake clothing such as your children's christening gowns in acid-free tissue before storing them in a cedar chest or trunk. Don't store these in your basement if it's damp there because moisture could damage the items.

 Encourage your kids to be neater. Show them how to arrange their clothes on rods and shelves by color. It's pleasing to the eye and tends to help them be neater.

Lighten Up

Mood lighting is lovely, but not when it's created by a layer of dust. Clean lighting fixtures, including the base, shade, and bulbs regularly. Consider installing a dimmer for that soft glow you want when it's just you and your partner enjoying an evening in.

 Avoid buying lacquered lamp bases if you have kids. Too-frequent touching and dusting may damage the surface.

Employ extra vigilance if you want ceiling fan-light combos. The blades tend to pick up dust, as do the bulbs, so don't forget them when dusting.

 Choose bulbs according to the kind of light you need in the area. Also consider costs. Incandescent bulbs offer a soft glow and ambience for dining areas. Fluorescent bulbs are money savers—they last up to 20 times longer than incandescent bulbs with four times the light. They're great in study and work areas. Halogen bulbs are both powerful and energy saving. They give up to three times as much light and last twice as long as incandescent bulbs.

 Clean brass lamp bases one of two different ways. For a shine use brass polish that contains wax. For a softer patina use one without wax.

 Get electrostatic dusters and feather dusters for cleaning ceiling, track, and canister lights, as well as difficult-to-reach sconces. To encourage kids to dust, buy them low-cost feather dusters in bright colors—and let them pick their favorites.

Wash removable shades in warm water with mild detergent. Try this on a small, hidden area first if you're not sure how this will affect the shade.

Let Me Entertain You

When furnished with oversize, comfy sofas and chairs; good lighting; an entertainment center holding a TV, DVDs, stereo, books, and games; and side tables, the living room is a great place to relax and entertain friends. No doubt, it's one of your kids' favorite places to camp out. The following page gives ways to keep it presentable.

Go for plain furniture as long as kids are in your house. Upholstered furniture, pillows, and window treatments often have decorative trim that can easily look bedraggled with lots of wear.

 Clean entertainment centers made of veneers by treating them according to the type of wood in the veneer. Wipe up water spills immediately.

 Wipe DVDs and CDs in a straight line from the center out, not in a circle that can scratch. Use a damp, lint-free cloth. Show your kids how to do this and explain that improper care can ruin the CDs they have.

 Clean the optical mechanism inside a compact disc player with a CD lens cleaner monthly to keep it dust-free.

 Dust the TV screen with a dry, soft cloth or one dampened with window cleaner. Vacuum the vents monthly.

 Position pianos away from air conditioners, heat vents, and direct sunlight.

 Clean pianos with a flick of a feather duster (call your kids in again!) followed by a damp cotton cloth in the direction of the wood grain. Wipe away any moisture.

DID YOU KNOW?

Ives McGaffey patented the first vacuum cleaner. Calling it the "Whirlwind," he built it in his home in Chicago in 1869. It was an instant success, and no wonder. Prior to this, carpets had to be hauled out of homes to be beaten or shaken. This sight was a sure sign of spring cleaning.

Reading Matters

If you're lucky enough to have a library, you want to take care of the books in it. The following tips work just as well for books there, as on any other shelf in your house. And it's good to get the children accustomed to taking care of their books now because they'll be responsible for them at least through college.

 Store books where air circulates. Moisture, excessive dryness, and humidity can destroy them.

 Remove odors from leather-bound books by placing them in a paper bag with baking soda. Shake the bag several times and let it be for a week. Then remove the books and shake them well.

 Routinely dust both shelves and books because dust can attract moisture.

 Try a soft shaving brush to dust dirt off books. Always brush away from the spine.

 Position bookshelves away from sunlight, spotlights, and fluorescent lighting, which can fade them.

 Use sturdy shelves and don't pack them so tightly that it makes book retrieval difficult for you or for the kids.

Clear Tables

Too often the coffee table becomes the living room's dumping ground, the place where things are thrown simply because it's there. It's much better used to display neat stacks of magazines or small tablescapes of candles, figurines, or flowers.

Memo from mom

HELP FOR TEEN HAVOC

With two teens in the house, it seemed like a tornado struck every day. These kids never seemed to be home, but their rooms looked like a disaster occurred—loose papers, trash, and dirty clothes everywhere. Here's how I helped them to help themselves get organized and saved myself work too:

With my son:

• We hung a basketball hoop on the back of his door. Then he heaved his dirty laundry into his hoop. The basket underneath caught his "free throws."

• We installed a sports locker in the corner of the room. He kept his seasonal outerwear hanging in this instead of the overstuffed common coat closet at the front door.

With my daughter:

• Together we hung a soft-sided shoe rack on the back of her door that kept barrettes and hair bows organized and tidy.

• We tied a 1-inch-wide ribbon in a bow and nailed it to a bare wall with one 18-inch tail hanging down. On it she attached all those dance corsages. It makes great room décor, plus it keeps them organized.

—from Jana Finnegan, Norwalk, Iowa
A busy mom to Adam, 21 years old, and Briana, 18 years old

 TIP 373 **Tidy up** coffee tables at the end of each day. You'll wake up to a fresher-looking room and will be prepared for any unannounced visitors.

 TIP 374 **Limit** the number of breakables and knickknacks you have around, at least until the kids are out of the house.

TIP 375 **Clean** metal bases of tables between dustings with warm sudsy water.

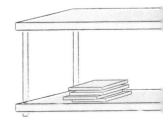

 TIP 376 **Put the overflow** of magazines and books in tidy piles underneath the coffee table.

Clean glass tops of coffee tables with a mixture of 2 tablespoons vinegar in 1 quart water. Moisten the cloth and wipe. Rinse with clear water and wipe dry with a cloth.

 Freshen up painted, varnished, or sealed wood tables with a sponge dipped in warm water and a mild detergent. Rinse and wipe dry immediately. Avoid abrasive cleansers that can damage the surface.

 Show kids how to remove candle wax from wood tops by heating it with a hair dryer set on medium. Warm the wax, then quickly wipe it off with a soft cloth or paper towel. Clean the area with a solution of mild distilled white vinegar and water.

Dining Rooms

Usually one of the most elegant rooms in the home, the dining room should also be comfortable and welcoming. It may even motivate you and your family to sit down together for a delicious meal every week or so.

Save care instructions for any items you buy and keep them in the linen closet for easy referral. If a fabric's fiber is unclear to you when at a flea market, ask. Antique items often need special handling.

 Save scorched linens by soaking in color-safe bleach and the hottest water safe for the fabric, followed by laundering.

 Clean fine linen or pieces with handmade lace, fringe or crocheted edging by presoaking in clear water. Then gently swish in warm water containing phosphate-free, mild detergent.

 Save steps by storing napery in a sideboard or armoire in the dining room.

Store tablecloths and napkins by the set. Add sachets or use scented shelf liners.

 Remove dust from lace curtains by tumbling them in the dryer on the air cycle. Many new lace curtains are hand or machine washable but always check the label first.

 Unroll bamboo shades and lay them flat before cleaning them. Weight each end, then wash with a sponge dipped in warm sudsy water. Rinse and hang to dry.

 Hand wash fiberglass shades from the '50s. It's easiest to do this in a large laundry tub filled with water and detergent. Rinse well.

Lighting Lore

The lighting we have in homes is important to create a mood as well as illumination. Old or new, hanging from the ceiling, standing on the floor, placed on a table, or affixed to a wall, light fixtures are one of the most important aspects of our decor.

 Turn off the electricity at the breaker box before cleaning sconces and track lighting. Wipe fixtures with a damp cloth. Dry thoroughly before turning the power back on.

 Brighten crystal chandeliers with a feather duster regularly.

 Dry-clean silk lampshades professionally before they begin to look dirty.

 Remove wax from new candlesticks, not antique copper or brass ones, by placing candlesticks upside down on a baking sheet and heating them briefly in the oven on the lowest temperature.

Don't use paper towels when cleaning candlesticks made of brass, silver, or another metal. Use a soft cloth.

 Clean glass or plastic globes by wiping them with a chamois cloth dampened with rubbing alcohol or paint thinner. Then buff them with a lint-free cloth.

Furniture Facts

Even start-up homes have some furniture. Care for it now, and you'll be able to hand it down to your children when they are ready to create their own households.

 Place tall case clocks—such as grandfather clocks—in corners far away from main traffic areas. Clock repair shops sell devices to secure them to the wall.

 Handle marquetry with care. These veneer surfaces inlaid with wood, shell, or ivory should be dusted gently, taking care not to catch the cloth on inlaid edges.

 Remove marks from candle wax and oils on your veneered and inlaid wood table by covering the marks thickly with talcum powder. Cover with several layers of paper towels and then iron with a warm, dry iron.

 Clean lacquered furniture with a damp cloth only when necessary and polish occasionally with furniture cream. A damp chamois cloth will remove finger marks.

Vacuum rugs with a beater brush. It will agitate the carpet fibers and loosen dirt so it's easily sucked away.

Dust the tops of picture frames and mirrors with the soft brush attachment of your vacuum cleaner.

For a Stylish Presentation

As any good hostess knows and is thankful for, even an average meal tastes better when it's served on beautiful china and eaten with gleaming silver. It's all about presentation. Details do make a big difference.

 Keep copper centerpieces and serving pieces away from moisture and humidity. Clean them with commercial copper polish.

 Remove tea and coffee stains on cups by rubbing them with a wet cloth dipped in dry baking soda or a salt-and-water paste.

 Wash old china by hand in warm, not hot, water. Don't soak pieces with gold glazes or trim because the water can lift off the glaze. Never put china in the dishwasher.

 Safely store china by placing paper plates, doilies, or paper towels between each piece. Keep stacks short so the weight of them won't cause damage.

 Avoid extreme temperatures with all glassware. For example, putting cold glasses into very hot water may cause them to break.

 Wash silver items by hand in warm, soapy water. The more they're used, the longer they'll stay shiny.

TIP 405 **Remove egg stains** from silver items by rubbing the piece gently with salt or a mixture of tomato juice and salt before washing it.

TIP 406 **Wait until items** are cool before removing from the dishwasher or having your kids help remove them. You could drop them or burn yourselves if they're too hot.

IMPORTANT WARNING: Be Alert to Inhalant Abuse

This drug is cheap, legal, and easy to get. It's in your kitchen, bathroom, office, and garage. And your school-age kids know all about it.

Inhalant abuse is easy to hide from unsuspecting parents.
Aerosols, fuels, and solvents are poisons when inhaled, but preteens and teens "sniff," "huff," or "bag" to get high. They don't realize a single episode of inhalant abuse, even the first episode, can be fatal almost instantly.

There are more than 1,000 products that are dangerous when inhaled. Commonly abused inhalants include compressed air used to clean computer parts and aerosol cans of whipped cream. Teenagers seek a "high" but the effects may deprive the brain and heart of oxygen.

Inhalant use may cause sudden death, even in healthy children. It can damage the brain, kidneys, and liver. These products can cause an addiction as difficult to treat as a cocaine addiction.

Commonly Abused Products

A recent study shows that 17 percent of eighth graders have abused inhalants. In other words, **by eighth grade one in five students will have used an inhalant to get high.** Using inhalants is most common in seventh to ninth graders. Immediately after school is the most popular time to use. Because most parents are unfamiliar with this form of drug abuse, they haven't warned their children about it.

The most commonly used products for inhalant abuse are:

- Model airplane glue
- Rubber cement
- Household glue
- Spray paint
- Hairspray
- Vegetable cooking spray
- Computer keyboard cleaner
- Nail polish remover
- Paint thinner
- Type correction fluid and thinner
- Gasoline
- Dry-cleaning fluid
- Video head cleaners
- Dessert topping spray

Here's what you can do:

- **Monitor the levels** of products that can be abused and how quickly your kids use them. How many cans of computer cleaner or spray paint does he or she go through in a month?

- **Watch for** the smell of products on their breath or clothes, slurred speech, chronic sore throats, and skin irritation, especially around their mouths. These are in addition to changes in behavior, poor school performance, and withdrawal from family and friends.

- **When you discuss** tobacco, alcohol, and other drugs with your children, discuss inhalants. Tell children these chemicals are poisons. These toxic substances can kill kids the first time they use them.

These websites offer parents and others helpful information on inhalant abuse:

- National Inhalant Prevention Coalition, www.inhalants.org
- National Institute on Drug Abuse, www.nida.nih.gov
- Substance Abuse & Mental Health Services Administration, www.samhsa.gov

Chapter 7

Clean It Green

"You must be the change you wish to see in the world."

—Mahatma Gandhi, spiritual leader of India

Everyone wants the world to be a healthy place to live, for themselves and their children, not just today, but in the years to come. The good news is that we can help achieve this by starting now in our own homes. It's generally not more difficult or expensive to clean green. And you'll have no worries that your cleaning agents will harm your kids or pets with chemical additives. In this chapter you'll discover:

- Why cleaning green is worth the effort
- How to find ready-made green cleaning products
- How to make your own green cleaners with ordinary household items

What Does "Green" Mean?

There are many cleaning products available today that claim to be environmentally safe, using words such as biodegradable, green, and nontoxic. That sounds good, but sometimes it's misleading. Just because the label says "natural" and has a drawing of the earth on it does not guarantee it to be a green product. In general, green cleaning is cleaning to protect health without harming the environment.

Why Should You Be Concerned?

According to the Worldwatch Institute, a nonprofit, environmental and social research organization in Washington, D.C., "Of the more than 2.4 million human toxic exposures reported to U.S. poison control centers in 2004, 93% occurred at a residence, and just over half (51.3%) occurred in children under six."

Cleaning substances are the second largest category of toxic exposures for children under six, after cosmetics and personal care products. Of the 121,197 reported exposures to household cleaning products in children in this age category in 2004, the majority (18%) were from bleaches, followed by wall/floor/tile cleaners (15%), automatic dishwasher detergents (10%), glass cleaners (7%), and disinfectants (7%)."

What Can You Do?

Ironically, many products that clean our homes pollute our environment. Fortunately, now you don't have to choose between a clean home and a safe environment and you can save money at the same time. Here are some tips to help you clean green from Earth Share, a nonprofit organization.

• **Use water- or vegetable-base** paints, stains, and varnishes. If you have leftover paint thinners, household cleaners, oil, or pesticides, never pour them down the drain; they can pollute the water supply. Instead call your local city hall to find out the next date when hazardous waste will be collected.

• **Don't sand or burn off paint** that may contain lead. Lead particles in the paint can cause lead poisoning. If your paint is peeling, use a wet sponge or mop to clean up the debris instead of sanding. Never vacuum the dust or chips from lead paint; it will only disperse more lead dust into the air.

• **Get rid of the junk** in your garage or attic. Talk to your neighbors and organize a community yard sale. You can foster neighborhood relationships, earn extra cash, and help save the environment at the same time. If a yard sale seems like too much work, donate your giveaways to your local nonprofit thrift store.

• **Pay attention** to your water bill. Wasted water hurts the environment and your checkbook. Always fix leaky faucets in your house immediately. A 5-minute repair project can often save gallons of water. You can also place a large rock in a toilet tank to save water when flushing. Be sure to check hoses and sprinklers periodically and fix any leaks. See the next page for more green cleaning tips.

Choose cleaning products that are nontoxic, biodegradable, phosphate free, and chlorine free.

 Use natural fiber sponges.

 Reduce paper use. Use rags instead of paper towels and cloth napkins instead of paper napkins.

 Insulate windows, doors, attics, and crawlspaces against drafts. Earth Share says that if all windows in the United States were energy efficient, we would save up to 2.5 percent of the total amount of energy we consume each year.

 Check for an energy-efficiency label when you're buying appliances. Many new appliances come with an Energy Efficiency Rating (EER). The higher the EER, the less it will cost you to operate the appliance.

 Adjust air conditioning and heating thermostats to use less energy when you're not home or sleeping. When you're at home during the summer, 78° F is a comfortable, energy-efficient temperature.

 Keep your cooling system well maintained. Call a professional to check it at least once a year.

 Wrap your water heater in an insulated jacket. You can reduce carbon dioxide emissions by up to 4,000 pounds a year and save on your water bill too.

 Turn off unneeded lights and appliances.

ADVICE FROM THE EXPERT

Annie B. Bond, executive producer of .Care2.com's *Healthy Living Channel*, says, "Finding your way to a home of healing energy is a path of discovery and reward. Some people remove all of their toxic household products and replace them with safe alternatives overnight. Others prefer the step-by-step approach."

Here are easy ways to transition to a natural lifestyle:

1. **Choose the least toxic,** most natural alternative every time you buy anything, be it a couch, peach, shampoo, or furniture polish.

2. **Go back** to naturally derived ingredients to make cleaning products that work, don't pollute, and save you money.

3. **Mix and match** effective homemade formulas with a few well-chosen commercial brands. Natural cleaning products cost about one-sixth of comparable commercial products, so you'll do your budget a favor too.

Stock Green Products

Keep green products on hand in your closets and cupboards. Hang a magnetized list on the door and jot down supplies when you're running low so you can keep track of what you need to replenish.

 TIP 416 **Use** the following as green cleaning items: baking soda, white vinegar, cornstarch, baby powder, liquid castile (vegetable-base) and neutral-pH soap, toothpaste, borax, scouring pads, cotton washcloths and rags, old socks, T-shirts, cotton and woolen gloves, and paper towels made from recycled paper.

TIP 417 **Use foods** and spices to clean too. These include: lemons, oranges, bread, seltzer, club soda, olive oil, coffee grounds, apple cider vinegar, fresh herbs, essential oils, salt, and tap water.

General Cleansers

Most of the green cleaning "recipes" consist of only two ingredients and require mixing them into a liquid or paste. Once you try these, you'll probably like them and use them frequently. Here are a few basic ones:

Liquid soap: Mix 1/4 cup glycerin soap flakes with 3/4 cup boiling water until dissolved. If the soap hardens over time, simply reheat and add water until the mixture attains its original consistency.

Gentle Cleaner: Sprinkle 1 tablespoon of baking soda on a damp rag. Add a little liquid soap to the rag and rub the dirty area. Rinse well.

Scouring Powders: Sprinkle baking soda or borax on the dirty surface and scour with a damp cloth, then rinse. Or shake salt on the surface, then clean with a cloth dipped in lemon juice. Wipe clean with a water-dampened cloth.

Window Wonders

There are many simple ways to clean windows green and save time and money. For example:

TIP 418 **Avoid streaks** when cleaning your windows. Add a dash of liquid detergent to a mild water and vinegar solution. On the next page are three potential green window cleaning solutions you can make.

Recipe #1: Mix 2 tablespoons household ammonia or white vinegar with 1 quart warm water.

Recipe #2: Mix 2 tablespoons rubbing alcohol with 1 cup white vinegar.

Recipe #3: Blend a mixture of half white vinegar and half warm water.

Curtains and Draperies

 Take cotton drapes out of the dryer before they're completely dry. Stretch them gently and then hang them. No ironing needed—you'll save energy and time.

 Avoid curtains that extend into "puddles" on the floor. They may look beautiful, but they're terrible dust trappers.

BEAT THE CLOCK

1. Make enough of your favorite natural cleaning solution to fill a 16-ounce spray bottle. Its shelf life is about 4 to 6 months when stored in a cool, dark place.

2. Dab or soak stains with ice-cold water before using any commercial solutions. You may not even need the commercial products!

3. Use a rolling lint remover to dust fabric lampshades, the tops of curtains, or any difficult place to reach.

4. Clean up as you go along and you won't have to do it when you're finished.

Bust Those Dust Bunnies

Give your home that fresh lemony fragrance by turning an ordinary dust cloth into something extraordinary. All you need are 2 or 3 tablespoons of lemon juice and a bowl of water. Combine the lemon juice with the water, soak the cloth, wring it out well, and then dust. You can also add some jojoba or linseed oil—natural moisturizers are good for wood. Let the cloth dry before using. Store solutions in a sealed container.

Do Wonders for Walls

Basic cleaner: Mix 1 gallon water with 1 cup apple cider vinegar. Wipe the walls and washable wallpaper a small section at a time.

Basic stain remover: A paste of equal parts baking soda and water usually does the trick.

Cleaner for oil-base painted walls: Combine 2 tablespoons of vinegar with 1 quart of warm water.

Cleaner for textured oil-base painted walls: Wash with a solution of 1 ounce borax to 1 pint water. Rinse with clear water.

Cork cleaner: Treat cork with a polyurethane sealer once it's installed. Then it can be cleaned with a solution of 2 tablespoons distilled white vinegar to 1 gallon water.

Clean Those Carpets

Cleaner: Sprinkle dry cornstarch on the carpet, wait half an hour, and then vacuum.

Freshener: Mix 1 cup baking soda with ½ cup crushed lavender flowers. Mix well. Sprinkle it on carpets liberally. Let it sit for 30 minutes before vacuuming.

Revitalizer: Mix 1 cup white vinegar and 2½ cups warm water. Spray a fine mist of it on the carpet. Scrub the area lightly with a brush. Let it dry.

Sift 1½ cups baking soda, 2 tablespoons cornstarch, and 3 drops vanilla essential oil together with a hand sifter. Sprinkle it over the dry carpet and let set for 2 hours before vacuuming.

Work on Wood Floors

Polish #1: Mix 1 tablespoon beeswax in 2 cups of mineral oil. Heat the mixture in a double boiler to melt the wax and blend ingredients. Apply the cooled solution to floors with a soft cloth.

Polish #2: Brew two tea bags in 1 quart of boiling water and let the mixture cool to room temperature. Mop the floor with the solution. No need to rinse.

Keep Furniture Fabulous

Dust your furniture appropriately on a regular basis and you won't have to polish it too often.

Bamboo: A soft damp cloth is the best way to keep this furniture clean.

Cane: Clean it by wiping well with a soft dry cloth.

Oak and mahogany: Wipe these woods with a cloth dipped in warm beer and wrung out well. Maybe this is a task your life partner may enjoy.

Plastic laminate: Rub it with a damp cloth that has been dipped in baking soda.

Scratches: Mix equal parts of lemon juice and vegetable oil. Rub into the scratches with a soft cloth until scratches disappear.

DID YOU KNOW?

Never mix ammonia with chlorine bleach. The combination creates a reaction that yields chlorine gas, which is a deadly poison.

<u>Unfinished wood:</u> Apply a small amount of mineral oil on a cloth and rub.

<u>Wicker:</u> Brush or vacuum it regularly. Wash pieces with sudsy water and borax. If the piece is really dirty, add a capful of ammonia and rinse well.

<u>Wood:</u> Combine ½ cup canola oil, ¼ cup liquid soap, and ½ cup water. Shake well. Apply it with a soft cloth and buff to a shine. Dry outside on a sunny day for an extra-fresh scent.

Upkeep Upholstered Furniture

To keep fabric bright, vacuum upholstered pieces monthly. If cushions are unlined and filled with down, brush them instead of vacuuming them, as that may draw out feathers. Here are other ways to keep upholstered pieces looking good for a long time:

 Use washable slipcovers in the summer when guests and family might plop down damp from the beach or perspiration. If this isn't possible, protect furniture with throws made of sheets that coordinate and can be thrown in the washer and dryer.

 Iron cotton and linen slipcovers by pressing them on the wrong side while they're still damp. Put covers on cushions and furniture immediately so they'll conform to the furniture's original shape while still in a flexible mode.

 Make upholstery shampoo by combining ¼ cup liquid dish detergent or laundry detergent with 1 cup warm water (be sure to test it first where is doesn't show. If it does leave a ring, it won't be noticeable). It may be worth the money to have good pieces professionally cleaned once a year.

Memo from mom

MOM IN MAINE GOES GREEN

Cleaning green and recycling are great ways to teach kids about saving the planet. Here are some good ideas for you:

- **Use a bit of ground coffee** in an open container to deodorize the refrigerator.
- **Stash empty cologne bottles** in the corner of your closet shelf so that your clothes will take on your favorite scent. It's a great way to recycle.
- **Clean a crusty microwave oven** the easy way. I bring a bowl of water to a boil (you can add lemon juice or baking soda to the water to deodorize it). Let the water stand a couple of minutes, then remove the bowl and wipe out the oven with a damp sponge.

—Debbie Burleson, Bath, Maine
A busy mom to Miles, 14 years old, and Kate, 15 years old

Use Unusual Items to Clean Green

Ta-dah! Who would have thought your old wool cardigan could be useful for cleaning? But it's true. It's just one of many items everyone has that is multifunctional. Not only does it clean well, but by reusing it, you're recycling in the best possible way, and often decluttering, too.

Corner cleaners: Use an old regular toothbrush, tired-out toothbrush head of an electric toothbrush, or cotton swabs to get dirt out of windowpane corners.

Window washing items: Use old sponges, T-shirts, or the squeegee you use for your car windshield to wash windows. These low-cost items work really well.

Screen savers: Prior to washing window screens, brush them with a vacuum cleaner brush or any stiff-bristled brush.

Nonwashable wallpapered walls: Try a gum eraser or lump of stale rye bread. Gently rub the wall with a downward movement, not up or sideways. As the eraser or bread picks up the dirt, turn it so you're always using a clean side.

Grease spots on wood furniture: As soon as possible, pour salt on the grease to absorb and prevent staining. Carefully wipe it away.

Water spots on wood furniture: Rub gently with toothpaste applied to a damp cloth.

Clean large things outside: If you have a patio, garden, yard, or driveway, outside is the best place to wash screens, removable windows, garden furniture, and other bulky pieces. Lay the item on the ground, previously covered with a large plastic sheet, or on a picnic table. Rinse with the garden hose after scrubbing with soapy water. Prevent streaks by shaking off the excess water, then wiping items down with a clean cloth soaked in rinse water and squeezed well.

Phooey to fingerprints: Roll up a slice of white bread and dab firmly on the marks.

DID YOU KNOW?

The Environmental Protection Agency (EPA) suggests shoppers read product labels carefully, looking especially for "signal words" that indicate how dangerous or toxic a product can be.

*The most toxic products will be marked with the signal words, "**Danger-Poison**" and the skull-and-crossbones symbol. Moderately toxic items will carry the word "Warning." Slightly toxic products will use the word "Caution."*

Read labels carefully for precautionary and first-aid measures, as well as handling and storage instructions, all of which should be followed exactly.

Would You Believe...

That you can safely polish fine silver with toothpaste? Yes, it's true, and it creates a beautiful shine. That wonder product of all time, baking soda, also works well, especially on badly tarnished pieces. Simply make a paste of baking soda with water, apply to the silver, and leave it on for an hour. Remove the paste gently with a sponge and hot water. Dry and burnish silverware with a soft, clean cloth.

Bathrooms

Used countless times during the day and night and seen most often by guests, bathrooms need cleaning more often than any other room in the house. Plus, they can attract mold and mildew, along with germs and bacteria, none of which are good for your family's well-being. Here are green cleaning alternatives:

Antibacterial spray: Tea tree, lavender, eucalyptus, and sandalwood are all known to have antiseptic (antibacterial, disinfectant, antimicrobial, germicidal) qualities. Combine a small amount of any of them in oil with water in a spray bottle. Shake it well and use.

Germicide: Mix ½ cup borax with 1 gallon hot water. Add a few sprigs of fresh thyme or rosemary and steep for 10 minutes. Strain and cool before using. Store in and use from a plastic spray bottle.

Conquer Mold and Mildew

The basics: Keep surfaces dry, fix leaks, dry out carpets, and make sure shower curtains keep water in the tub and not on the floor. Wipe up spills quickly.

Ceramic tiles: Wash these with warm water and a few drops of dishwashing detergent. Rub soap-splattered tiles with a cut lemon. Leave the lemon juice on for 15 minutes and then polish with a soft cloth.

Easy clean: The simplest way to remove mold is to use straight vinegar (it's a weak acid—that's why it works so well). Spray it on and let it do its thing. The odor will dissipate in a few hours.

Green Kitchen Tips

Keeping the kitchen clean comes naturally. You're always there (or so it seems), and it's filled with items that are as good for cleaning as they are for cooking. Baking soda, white vinegar, and lemon juice make up the triumvirate that cleans almost anything. Keep them handy and this will be the freshest room in the house. Now if you could just bottle a chef.

Countertop: Mix 1 cup liquid soap, $\frac{1}{4}$ cup freshly squeezed lemon juice, $\frac{1}{4}$ eyedropper tea-tree extract, and 6 cups warm water. Place the solution in a plastic spray bottle, spray on the countertop, and wipe off.

Cutting board: Combine essential oils made from any of the natural disinfectants listed in the Bathroom section with water in a spray bottle. Shake well and spritz. Let the area dry without wiping, or let it set 15 minutes before drying with a clean cloth.

Drains: Pour $\frac{1}{4}$ cup baking soda down the clogged drain followed by $\frac{1}{2}$ cup of vinegar. Close the drain tightly until the fizzing stops, then flush with boiling water.

Microwave: Combine 2 tablespoons baking soda or lemon juice with 1 cup water. Place the mixture in a microwave-safe bowl. Allow the mixture to boil for 5 minutes or until steam condenses on the walls and door. Remove the bowl and wipe down the interior with a clean cloth.

Mineral deposits: Rub vinegar onto the brownish stain that forms where a faucet drips or the water drains away. If the stain persists, put paper towels soaked in vinegar on the stain and let them set overnight.

Oven: Make a paste of baking soda, salt, and hot water. Use with a stiff brush or steel wool.

Pots and pans: Generously sprinkle bottom of pots and pans with water; cover the burned food with enough baking soda so that the surface is completely white. Sprinkle a bit more water on the top. Let the mixture sit overnight. Usually the burnt food can be lifted right out. Any residue can be removed with concentrated scrubbing.

Safe Laundry Helpers

There's something satisfying about doing the wash, folding everything neatly, and putting it all away (or even better, getting the kids to do it). Add to this the use of products that don't pollute the environment or harm the family, and the chore that never goes away gets a whole lot better.

Fabric softener: Add ½ to 1 cup vinegar in the rinse cycle if you wash with soap or ½ cup baking soda in the wash cycle.

Spray starch: Mix 1 tablespoon cornstarch with 1 pint cold water. Using a pump spray bottle, spray on clothes while ironing.

Static-cling prohibiter: Toss a small wet towel into the dryer a few minutes before the end of the cycle.

USE CAUTION

Although the ingredients you use to make green cleaners may be of organic origin, including edible items such as lemons and olive oil, that doesn't mean they're without consequences. Exercise the same caution with them as with any commercial cleaner. Keep them away from children and pets, don't let anyone or anything drink or eat them, and take care that they don't get in the eyes.

Natural Bug and Rodent Repellants

Regardless of how clean and tidy a person may be, nearly everyone's home gets visited by creepy crawlies sometime or other. It could be the weather, underground construction in the neighborhood, or a million other little things that cause their arrival. Rather than use harmful chemicals, get rid of them in an environmentally correct, child-safe way. Here are some methods that really work:

Ants: Deter ants by sprinkling a few crumbled bay leaves on windowsills. Place whole bay leaves in sugar, cereal, and flour containers. Ants also seem to dislike red chili pepper, vinegar, orange and lemon peels, salt, and instant grits (even the ants up north).

Earwigs: They prefer moist, shady places such as wood piles and flowerpots, and cracks and crevices around baseboards. Catch them by rolling up a newspaper, dampening it, and placing it near their suspected hiding place.

Mice: Hang sprigs of mint in kitchen cabinets and cupboards or place mint leaves on shelves. Rub the leaves often to release their scent.

Spiders: Capture spiders by inverting a glass over them and sliding a stiff piece of paper under the glass. After trapping, let them loose outside. Spiders are important participants in our ecosystem, so killing them is not good for anyone. Your kids might enjoy helping you with this chore.

Harmless Pet Pampering

Our furry friends are the best! But they can make messes and create bad smells. The more natural the products used for them and everything they come in contact with, the healthier they (and you) will be. Here are green pet cleaning tips:

To eliminate odors on the carpet where accidents have happened, mix 1 cup vinegar, ½ cup baking soda, and 4 cups water. Apply, let dry, then vacuum. Add 1 teaspoon vanilla or pineapple essential oil for an extra-nice scent.

 Get rid of pet odor on hardwood floors by mixing equal amounts of water and white vinegar. Wipe the mixture sparingly on the spot and let set for up to 1 hour. Rinse and mop. Note that the vinegar may remove some of a wax finish, so you'll need to rewax the area.

 Make litter box deodorizer by mixing 1 teaspoon baking soda into kitty litter. Measure the baking soda carefully—too much may keep your cat away.

 Keep dogs' coats shiny with a rinse made from ½ cup fresh or dried rosemary mixed with 1 quart boiling water. Let the mixture steep for 20 minutes, then strain and cool. Massage into his or her coat and skin. Let your pet air dry or you'll remove the scent.

 Control fleas in pet beds by cutting a purchased flea collar into four to six pieces. Place them underneath the bed itself or under the cushion if it is removable.

 Mix garlic into your pet's food to repel fleas. The odor will permeate the skin, and fleas don't like it. Or put lemon slices in boiling water, let cool, and spray your pet with it two to three times weekly.

 Scatter a light layer of borax on your carpet and leave it for an hour. Follow with a thorough vacuuming to discourage fleas.

Sprinkle baking soda on pets' beds and around them to remove odors. Let the soda sit for 15 minutes and then vacuum.

 Remove skunk spray odor from pets by bathing them in a mixture of 1 part organic apple cider with 2 parts water. Be careful not to get this in their eyes because it may sting.

TIP 433 **Wrap your hand** with wide packing tape if a lint brush isn't handy to remove pet hair from anything and everything. Another way to pick up pet hair is to put on a rubber glove and dampen it. When you rub the glove against fabric, the hair will stick to the glove. Test this first on an inconspicuous area of the garment or piece of furniture to make sure the dampness doesn't leave a spot.

Four Reasons Green Is Better

According to Denise Dochnahl, marketing specialist of Simple Green, a manufacturer of nontoxic, biodegradable, environmentally sensitive cleaning products, there are many reasons to choose a "green" cleaning product:

1. **Ease and value:** One bottle of a nontoxic, concentrated, all-purpose cleaning product can be used in a multitude of ways.

2. **Safety:** If you have children, you most definitely want to use nontoxic cleaning products. Ingestion accidents happen in the home all the time despite the diligence of moms everywhere. Babies and children come into direct contact with household surfaces every day and also with whatever cleaning chemicals used there.

3. **Environmental considerations:** All you have to do is contact the manufacturer to find out if a product contains plant or animal ingredients. Those without them are better for allergy and asthma sufferers. You also want to look for readily biodegradable products, meaning that they break

down at an appropriate rate, not too fast and not too slowly. Nontoxic and readily biodegradable products are septic safe. Also look for products that are phosphate free, so they don't build up in waterways and cause eutrophication (the creation of a deficiency in dissolved oxygen).

4. Your legacy: You'll leave a less-polluted world for your children and for your children's children.

No Hassle Green Living

Besides cleaning green, Moms everywhere are considering living green as a plus for themselves, their life partners, and their children. During the last half century, synthetic, manufactured chemicals have made their way into our homes and cupboards.

It's important to check labels—have your kids help—and avoid products with additives. Teach your kids how to recycle paper and why it's important. Explain how some pesticides and herbicides may be harmful. Show them living green can be healthful and fun.

 Serve fresh fruits and vegetables instead of canned ones whenever possible. The fresh foods taste better and don't contain salt or additives, which can be harmful.

 Get a water filter installed to purify your family's water supply.

 Ask for "green" or "earth-friendly" building supplies if you're tackling a building or remodeling project. They're now available at many home improvement stores.

 Don't use products made of plastic foam. They contain suspected carcinogens and hormone disrupters that can harm humans—and children in particular.

Chapter 8

Create an Allergy-Free Kid Zone

" The greatest wealth is health."
—*Virgil, poet of Ancient Rome*

Today it's estimated that 2 million children have some type of allergy. That accounts for the loss of an estimated two million school days per year. Besides keeping your children from attending school, allergies can make them miserable with runny noses, itchy eyes, sore throats, and skin rashes. Things such as dust, dogs, cats, birds, and cockroaches in the home can cause allergies.

Dust mites are one of the most common causes of children's allergies, and the main allergic component of house dust. Present year-round in most parts of the United States, although not at high altitudes, dust mites live in bedding, upholstery, and carpets.

According to Jeffrey D. Miller M.D., Danbury, Connecticut, a clinical allergist, dust mite researcher, and president of Mission: Allergy, Inc., "Dust mites avoid the light and need at least 50 percent relative humidity to survive." He says there are five easy ways to decrease dust mite exposure throughout the home:

1. If it's a hard surface, wipe it.
2. If it's a washable fabric, wash it in hot water.
3. If you can't wipe or wash it, encase it.
4. If you can't wipe, wash, or encase it, remove it.
5. If indoor air is damp, monitor it, and keep relative humidity below 45 percent by using air-conditioning or a dehumidifier, and avoid humidifiers. ° ©Mission: Allergy, Inc., used with permission.

What Causes Allergies?

- **Molds,** another common allergen, are fungi that thrive indoors and out in warm, moist environments. In the home they can thrive in poorly ventilated places such as the bathroom. Molds tend to be seasonal but can grow year-round, especially those indoors.

- **Pet allergens** are dispersed when the pet licks itself and the saliva gets on its fur or feathers. As the saliva dries, protein particles become airborne and work their way into fabrics in the home. Cats are the worst because they lick themselves frequently as part of their grooming.

- **Cockroaches** are especially prevalent in cities. Exposure to them is thought by many to be a major cause of asthma.

Here are some tips for helping your child avoid airborne allergens:

 Remove carpets or rugs from your child's room. Hard floor surfaces don't collect dust as much as carpets, thereby decreasing the possibility, and number, of dust mites.

 Don't hang heavy drapes that attract dust. Get rid of other items that accumulate dust. Use special covers to seal pillows and mattresses.

 Keep your child's bedroom windows closed when the pollen season is at its peak.

 Change childrens' clothing after being outdoors and don't let them mow the lawn. (They'll be so disappointed.)

 Have your child avoid damp areas such as basements if he or she is allergic to mold.

 Clean the entire house frequently and keep bathrooms and other mold-prone areas clean and dry.

Prepare the Bedrooms

If your child is dust sensitive, or has allergies or asthma, you can reduce his or her misery by creating a "dust-free" bedroom. By following the routine suggested by the National Institute of Allergy and Infectious Diseases as described below, you can also help reduce exposure to cockroaches and other bugs.

Although these steps may seem difficult at first, experience plus habit will make them easier. The results—better breathing, fewer medicines, and greater freedom from allergy and asthma attacks—will be well worth your effort.

- Completely empty the room.
- Empty and clean all closets and if possible, store the contents elsewhere and seal the closets.
- Keep clothing in zippered plastic bags and shoes in boxes off the floor if you can't store them elsewhere.
- Remove carpeting if possible.
- Clean and scrub the woodwork and floors thoroughly to remove all traces of dust.
- Wipe wood, tile, or linoleum floors with water, wax, or oil.
- Cement any linoleum to the floor.
- Close the doors and windows until the dust-sensitive person is ready to use the room.

TIP 444 **Wear** a filter mask when cleaning.

TIP 445 **Air and clean** the room thoroughly once a week.

Clean floors, furniture, tops of doors, window frames, and windowsills with a damp cloth or oil mop.

 Vacuum carpet and upholstery regularly.

TIP 448 **Wash curtains** often at 130°F.

Memo from mom

HANDY HELPERS

I think it's the little things that help out the most when cleaning. Whether it's a little assistance from your daughter or advice from a good friend, these handy helpers will save you time and effort.

1. Use a scrub brush for simple jobs. When the shower curtain needs cleaning, spread it on the grass outside and give your daughter a scrub brush, mild soap, and the garden hose, and let her slip-and-slide it clean.

2. Keep a small dustpan and brush handy for sweeping up dry spills—cereal, flour, coffee, cat food, etc. Children like to do this.

3. Have two vacuum cleaners—one for upstairs, another for downstairs. It prevents you from having to lug them up and down.

4. Fold plastic grocery bags into small triangles à la origami to store neatly for reuse. Our friend Akiko Keener taught us how:

- Smooth and flatten the bag, straightening handles and side pleats neatly.
- Fold bag in half lengthwise, smooth, and fold again so bag is long and slender.
- Neatly flag fold the bag, starting at the bottom, up to the handles and tuck the last little bit of the handles into the top fold.

—*from Gabriella Kaye, North Stonington, Connecticut*
A mom to grown-up daughter Anna

ADVICE FROM AN EXPERT—
ACUPUNCTURE FOR ALLERGIES

According to Naomi Rabinowitz, MD, the Medical Director of Turning Point Acupuncture in New York City:

Traditional Chinese Medicine (TCM) views all medical problems as the result of an imbalance or disharmony in our body's life force energy, known as Qi (pronounced "chee"). The energy imbalances can arise from external (environmental) or internal causes. The science and art of TCM is to identify the exact nature of the Qi disharmony and then correct it through the use of acupuncture, herbal medical formulas, and dietary and lifestyle advice.

From a TCM point of view, **allergies may be caused by any one of a number of different patterns of energy imbalances.** Allergic symptoms related to deficient lung Qi are common in Western cultures, where little attention is paid to proper breathing. Additionally, the Western diet, with its predominance of overprocessed foods, fats, and sweets, can injure the underlying digestive Qi. Weak digestive Qi can manifest itself as phlegm and nasal discharge.

Allergic symptoms such as sneezing, runny nose, shortness of breath, itching, and associated fatigue usually respond well to acupuncture and Chinese herbs. However, it may take up to two months of weekly treatment to see significant, lasting results. Eastern exercise forms that emphasize breathing, such as Tai Qi, Qi Gong, and yoga, also help to build lung Qi and the body's defensive energy to prevent respiratory symptoms.

Treat Carpeting and Flooring

Carpeting makes dust control almost impossible. Although shag carpets are the worst type to have if you are dust sensitive, all carpets trap dust. Health care experts recommend hardwood, tile, or linoleum floors. Treating carpets with tannic acid can eliminate some dust mite allergens. Tannic acid, however:

- Is not as effective as removing the carpet
- Is irritating to some people
- Must be applied repeatedly

Prepare Beds and Furniture

 Keep only one bed in the bedroom. Most importantly encase the box springs and mattress in a zippered dust-proof, or allergen-proof, cover. Scrub bedsprings outside the room. If you must have a second bed in the room, prepare it in the same manner.

 Use only washable materials on the bed. Sheets, blankets, and other bedclothes should be washed frequently in water that is at least 130°F.

 Keep furniture and furnishings to a minimum.

 Avoid upholstered furniture and blinds.

 Use only a wooden or metal chair that you can scrub.

 Install only plain, lightweight curtains on the windows.

Control The Air

Air filters—either added to a furnace or a room unit—can reduce the levels of allergens. Electrostatic and HEPA (high efficiency particulate absorption) filters can effectively remove many allergens from the air. However, electrostatic filters may give off ozone, which can be harmful to your lungs if you have asthma.

A dehumidifier may help because dust mites need high humidity to live and grow. Clean the unit frequently with a weak bleach solution (1 cup bleach in 1 gallon water) or a commercial product to help prevent mold growth.

BEAT THE CLOCK

1. To avoid bathtub rings, don't use oily bath preparations. Use a water softener if you live in a hard-water area.

2. Initiate a no-food-no-drink policy in children's bedrooms. This will save you from cleaning up those icky spills.

3. Save time on pet care with a self-feeder/waterer. Depending on the number of pets you have, you'll only have to fill the feeder/waterer a couple days a week. If you have a cat, consider a self-cleaning litter box for the same reason.

4. Teach your kids how to make beds. Then have them do it daily as part of their morning routine. It doesn't have to be perfect, and you'll save time.

Watch the Toys

 Keep toys that will accumulate dust out of the child's bedroom.

 Avoid stuffed toys.

 Use only washable toys of wood, rubber, metal, or plastic.

 Store toys in a closed toy box or chest.

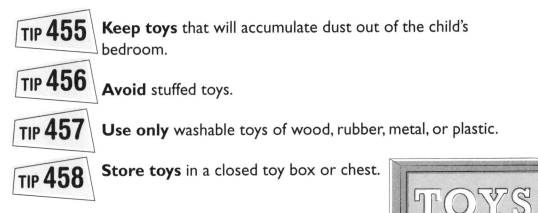

Reduce Reactions to Pets

Here's good news about pets and allergies: If you get a pet early in a child's life, it may prevent the same allergies the pet can cause. The Medical College of Georgia found that kids exposed to indoor pets from infancy were less than half as likely to develop allergies than kids not exposed to pets. However, if your children do have allergies to animals, here are tips:

 Keep the pet out of your children's bedrooms.

Designate one place for your pet to sleep and cover the area with a towel. Wash the towel weekly.

Try putting cheesecloth over your child's bedroom vent to keep out allergens.

Bathe, brush, and groom your pet regularly.

Have your children wash their hands and faces after petting or nuzzling an animal.

Consider Low Allergenic Cats and Dogs

If your children want a pet but you've ruled it out because one of them has allergies, take heart. Many kids with mild to moderate pet allergies can still snuggle up to a furry friend and enjoy the benefits of an animal companion.

While there are no "nonallergenic" breeds of dogs or cats, some are less likely than others to trigger an allergic reaction, says Dr. Anne Livingston, an allergist in Syracuse, New York. That's because some breeds produce less dander—the microscopic particles that can cause allergic reactions.

 You may want to get female, smaller dogs. They produce fewer allergens than large or male dogs.

 Research specific breeds that are better for kids with allergies. Some are the Basenji, the Soft-Coated Wheaten Terrier, Bichon Frise, Poodle, and Chinese Crested.

 Look into Labradoodles. They've been touted by many breeders as causing fewer allergies. So have other poodle mixes. However, it's best for you and your children to spend some time with one first to see how everyone reacts.

DID YOU KNOW?

Lillian Moller Gilbreth was not only the mother of 12 children, but an inventor, author, industrial engineer, and industrial psychologist. A pioneer in ergonomics, Gilbreth patented many kitchen appliances, including an electric food mixer, shelves inside refrigerator doors, and the famous trash can with a foot-pedal lid-opener.

TIP 467 **Consider** the Siberian, Devon rex, Cornish rex, and sphynx (a mostly hairless breed) if you're interested in adopting a cat. They're the best bets because they shed very little.

FOR MORE ALLERGY INFORMATION . . .

•Allergy & Asthma Network/Mothers of Asthmatics, 800-878-4403, www.aanma.org

•American Academy of Allergy, Asthma, and Immunology, 800-822-2762 / 414-272-6071, www.aaaai.org

•Asthma and Allergy Foundation of America, 800-7-ASTHMA / 800-727-8462, www.aafa.org

•National Institute of Allergy and Infectious Diseases (NIAID), 301-496-5717, www3.niaid.nih.gov/

•American Academy of Pediatrics, Children's Health Topics: Asthma & Allergies 847-434-4000, www.aap.org/healthtopics/asthma.cfm

•Mayo Clinic: Allergies www.mayoclinic.com/health/allergy/AA99999

•WebMD Inc. 212-624-3700, www.webmd.com/diseases_and_conditions/allergies.htm

•Pollen Count Indexes and Allergy Symptoms www.weather.com/activities/health/allergies/

Chapter 9

Don't Sweat the Pets

"Animals are such agreeable friends—they ask no questions, they pass no criticisms."
—George Eliot, Victorian novelist

Sure, Simbo the little kitty looked so adorable at the animal shelter that you and your kids just couldn't resist adopting him. But now he's taken to spraying your couch repeatedly, and you're getting desperate. Or you wanted a border collie so your kids could walk her and learn responsibility. But now no one does it, and poor Rosie just can't hold it all day. Don't despair, there are cures for accidents and other pet situations similar to this. The best cure of all is to be sure to train your pets correctly from the beginning to minimize accidents. Read on:

Preventive House-Training for Dogs

House-training is a defining moment in your relationship with your dog. Because elimination is a way to mark territory, teaching your dog where to eliminate confirms that you're the one in control. There are several types of training, but here we'll cover outdoor training and crate training.

Whatever type of house training is right for you and your dog, you'll need patience, persistence, and a good training plan. Stick with it. Your puppy wants to please you and will try his or her best to do whatever you ask.

Outdoor Training for Dogs

Here are the most important elements of successfully training your dog to eliminate outdoors. Remember that dogs are pack animals, and they respond to a hierarchy. You are the leader of the pack—you're the top dog who's in charge.

 Take your dog to a designated spot. When taking your dog out to eliminate, take him to the same place each time and say a short command, such as "Go" or "Do it."

 Let your puppy out to eliminate often. Puppies don't yet have much bladder control. As soon as the elimination is over, go back inside.

TIP 470 **Reward your puppy** after successful elimination with a healthy dog treat or extra praise and attention from you.

 TIP 471 **Keep a regular schedule.** A regular feeding, drinking, and elimination schedule is crucial to efficient house training. Daily feeding times should be consistent. About 15 to 20 minutes after a meal, take your dog outside to the elimination spot. Remove the dog's water a couple of hours before bedtime to reduce the need for late-night walks for elimination.

 TIP 472 **Confine your puppy** to a fenced-off area of your home, such as the kitchen, where you can watch it closely. This also discourages soiling; being den animals, dogs don't like to soil their playing and sleeping areas.

 TIP 473 **Observe your puppy** for the signs of a need to eliminate. Your puppy may head for a certain corner or go toward the door, for example. Once you know the signs, you can take your dog out immediately.

 TIP 474 **Put a leash** on your puppy when going outside to eliminate. A leash allows you to direct your dog to its elimination spot.

 TIP 475 **Praise your puppy** every time he or she relieves himself outdoors, particularly in the designated elimination spot.

 TIP 476 **Realize accidents** will happen. When your puppy has a lapse in judgment, say "No!" firmly and immediately take him or her to the outside elimination spot. Do not yell at, hit, or punish your puppy.

Dos and Don'ts of Crate Training

Dogs in the wild are den animals. Those instincts are in your puppy, so a crate is like a personal den. A crate provides a secure, comfy retreat from the household hubbub and a safe place to stay while you're away from home. Puppies are reluctant to soil their den, so being confined in a crate is a great way to prevent training accidents.

 Choose the correct size crate. A dog should have enough room to stand up, stretch, turn around, and lie down in the crate. If there is too much room, however, your dog will be tempted to use one end as an elimination spot. For large breeds, you may have to purchase two crates, a small one for the puppy and a larger one to accommodate your dog as it grows.

 Don't put food and water in the crate; your puppy's bladder and bowels will fill up, and he or she will have to eliminate in the crate.

 Say a single word such as "Kennel!" or "Crate!" to get your dog into the crate. Toss a dog toy into the crate. When your puppy enters, praise him and close the crate.

DID YOU KNOW?
Fun Dog Facts for Your Kids
- Most of the germs on a dog's tongue are not harmful to humans. You're more likely to get an illness from kissing a human than from kissing a dog.
- Your dog's sense of smell is 37 times more acute than yours.

Leave your puppy in the crate for 15 minutes to start with and gradually increase the time so that your puppy learns how to behave while you are away.

 Never let a puppy or adult dog spend most of the time crated. Dogs are pack animals and thrive on company.

 You'll learn how much crate time your dog is comfortable with. Some dogs can happily be crated while you're at work, and other dogs can only handle several hours in a crate, particularly if they are also crated at night.

Training Kitty to Use the Litter Box

Cats are naturally neat and intelligent, so it's generally not hard to teach them how to use a litter box. Some kittens will have learned this skill from their mothers, but if yours hasn't, don't worry. All it takes is a little practice on your pet's part and a little patience on yours to get this training down. If you're housebreaking an adult cat, the guidelines are the same, though it may be more challenging and take longer to change her ways.

Think Outside the Box

Start by picking a location for the litter box that your cat will approve of. Here are some tips:

 Provide privacy. Select a spot that's out of the flow of household traffic.

 Choose a quiet place. Noise can disrupt a kitten trying to concentrate. Pick a place away from chatty humans and loud appliances.

Locate the litter box a reasonable distance from your kitten's food and water dishes. (The opposite end of a room is OK; right next to the dishes is not.)

 Stay with the same spot. Moving the litter box from place to place might confuse your kitten and cause a setback.

Pick the Perfect Pan

Litter boxes come in many shapes, sizes, and materials. When selecting one for your kitten, look for one that's:

- **Easy to clean.** Plastic is the most practical material because it can be wiped down. A simple design will also make cleanups quick and painless. A covered box may help prevent messes if your kitten has poor aim or sends litter flying in all directions.

- **Sized for your kitten.** The box should provide ample room for your cat to find just the right place to do its business and to cover the resulting wet spots and droppings with litter. The box sides should be low enough for a small kitten or an older cat to easily climb in and out.

Litter Matters

Cat litter comes in various textures and scents. For a kitten's first litter, it's best to choose a basic, unscented kind; some kittens dislike scented litters and may refuse to use them. The litter can be either a traditional clay type or one of the newer clumping types, made to be scooped out as it's used instead of changed completely on a periodic basis.

Fill the box with about 3 inches of regular clay litter or 1-2 inches of clumping litter. Keep the box filled to this level so your cat always has enough litter to dig and paw.

Use Kitty-Friendly Techniques

Most cats who are provided with a clean, well-filled litter box will gravitate to it rather than use other surfaces in the home (with the possible exception of the soil in plant pots). You can help your kitten get the hang of using the box by doing the following:

 Be aware of the times your kitten is likely to need to use the box. These include after waking up, after eating, and whenever you see your cat sniffing around or squatting. At these times, gently scoop up your pet and carry her to the litter box to demonstrate the proper place to go.

 Pet your kitten and use lots of praise after he or she uses the litter box.

 Help your kitten associate pleasant experiences with using the box. Don't scold or say "no" to your cat, give any necessary medications, or do unpleasant grooming tasks when it's near the box.

DID YOU KNOW?
Fun Cat Facts for Your Kids

• A domestic cat's tongue feels like sandpaper. That's because the surface is covered with rasplike barbs that face backward. All cats use their tongues as a major grooming tool to clean and comb their fur.

• When your cat's tail quivers, it's the greatest expression of love he or she can give you.

Help for Litter Box Uh-Ohs

Once your kitten learns her litter-box lessons, she is unlikely to soil other parts of the house. If a house-trained cat starts avoiding her box, one of the following is usually to blame:

- **Did you change litter type,** scent, or brand? If you must introduce a new litter, start by mixing a little of the new filler in with the old and gradually increasing the proportion of the new kind.

- **Is the litter box scooped** often enough? Scoop out solid waste every day. If using clumping litter, scoop out the wet clumps daily as well. If using conventional litter, replace it completely once a week.

- **Is there too much noise** and activity around the litter box? Make sure the area near the box hasn't suddenly become busier.

- **Is it a territorial issue?** If a new cat joins the household, provide the newcomer with his or her own litter box. Unless they get used to using a box together at an early age, many cats balk at being asked to share this very private place with another animal.

Cleaning Up Puppy and Kitty Accidents

 Remove as much fresh urine as you can before it dries, especially from carpet. Place a thick layer of paper towels on the wet spot and cover that with a thick layer of newspaper. Stand on this padding for about a minute. Remove the padding and repeat the process until the area is barely damp.

 Be aware that products to combat odor may simply mask it, and in times of high humidity, the odor may reappear.

Put together a portable accident kit you can grab quickly to get to the soiled area before the stain sets. Include an enzyme cleaner, paper towels, plastic bags, and a spray bottle with a mild solution of dishwashing soap and water.

 Replace the damaged area of the carpet if the odor can't be removed. You or the store where you purchased your carpet may have scrap carpet you can use for this.

 You may need to also replace the carpet pad and even the subflooring if the urine has soaked through to it. Call a carpet professional for advice.

 Check with your carpet dealer about new carpet brands that resist spills and even prevent the spillage from soaking into the floor underneath.

 Remove solid waste right away. Don't scrub because that will further penetrate the carpet.

 Rinse the "accident zone" thoroughly with clean, cool water. After rinsing, remove as much of the water as possible by blotting or by using a wet/dry vacuum.

 Remove the old cleaner from the carpet first if you've previously used cleaners or chemicals of any kind on the area.

 Remove traces of old chemicals or clean old or heavy stains in carpeting by renting an extractor or wet/dry vacuum. These machines operate much like a vacuum cleaner, are efficient and economical, and do the best job of forcing clean water through your carpet and dirty water out. Be sure to follow the instructions carefully.

HOW TO CONTROL SHEDDING

Shedding is normal for most dogs and cats, but the extent and characteristics of shedding varies by breed attributes. Just like human hair, pets' hair grows and dies. Depending upon the breed, hair may shed easily. Normal shedding can't be stopped, but it can be controlled. Here's how:

1. Bathe, comb, and brush your pet as appropriate for the breed. (If you're unsure, call your veterinarian and ask.) This also prevents matted coats and promotes healthier skin when done right. (Note: Cats need baths very seldom—once a year if that—because they groom themselves regularly.) In general, short-haired cats shed less than long-haired breeds.

2. Start brushing or combing a new adult pet, puppy, or kitten slowly. Keep the sessions short and positive. Always stop before your pet protests.

3. Use healthy pet treats to help make the session pleasant. As your pet learns to enjoy the sessions, you can make them longer.

4. Call your veterinarian if heavy shedding is consistent throughout the year. Your pet may have a food sensitivity, dust allergy, or health problem and may need to be seen by a veterinarian.

Cat Breeds That Shed Little

- Cornish Rex
- Devon Rex

Dog Breeds That Shed Little

- Poodles
- Terriers
- Schnauzers
- Shih Tzus

Cleaning "Ooops" on Upholstery

 Remove waste from the area but do not smear the accident into the fabric.

 Gently blot the area with a paper towel.

 Sprinkle the area with baking soda to remove odors and absorb liquid. Vacuum up the baking soda after it dries.

 Test an inconspicuous area with water. If the fabric discolors, call a professional to deal with the pet stain and odor.

 Discourage your pet from using your bedding as a potty place by covering the bed with a vinyl, flannel-backed tablecloth. Or use plastic carpet runners with the pointy side up, available at home improvement stores.

 Make sleeping areas unappealing or unavailable by covering them with aluminum foil or plastic.

 You may find urine spots develop slowly after much time has elapsed. In beige carpet, blue dyes are attacked by pet urine, leaving behind the red and yellow dyes with a resulting stain appearing red, yellow, or orange. In cases such as these, consult a cleaning professional.

Avoid These Methods

TIP 507 — **Don't use** cleaning chemicals, especially those with strong odors such as ammonia or vinegar. They don't effectively eliminate or cover the urine odor—from your pet's perspective—and may encourage him to mark again in that area.

TIP 508 — **Never rub** the pet's nose in the soiled accident area. Too much time may have elapsed, and the pet may not even connect the accident with the gesture.

Can Your Kids Really Help With Pets?

"I promise I'll take care of him!" Children mean well, but they may not accurately gauge everything involved in taking care of pets.

Though you should encourage your children to participate in pet care, don't assume they'll be able to manage that responsibility on their own. Even teens may not be completely reliable when that favorite show comes on or when the person they're "going with" phones.

Most children will need adult supervision while caring for their pet, most of the time. As the parent, you determine which pet care tasks your children can handle. Here's what you can reasonably expect:

- **Starting around age 3,** young kids can help with feeding, watering, grooming, and walking. And of course, playing with your dog or cat is a great job for preschoolers; often the family pet is the only one who can keep up with them!

- **When they start school,** children can be assigned some pet care chores to do on their own, such as filling water bowls or giving the pet a daily brushing. A chore chart or other reminder system will go a long way toward making sure these tasks get accomplished.

- **Elementary school kids can** feed, water, groom, and play with a pet on their own, but under age 12 they shouldn't generally be allowed to walk a dog or cat (yes, cats can be taught to walk on a leash!) without an adult. Although it may depend on the size and age of the pet, for the most part preteens do not have the maturity to deal with the unexpected—such as another dog who may be aggressive or what to do if the pet slips its lead.

- **A 10-year-old** may be able to handle walking a cat, 15-pound miniature poodle, or even a slightly larger pet who's old and docile, but not a 100-pound German shepherd. Base your decision on the dog-to-child size ratio and your child's personal level.

- **Some teenagers** can handle full responsibility for a pet, from cleanup to vet care. Any responsibility a teen is willing and able to take on should be encouraged and supported.

Teach Children to Handle Pets Safely

1. **Explain to your children** how fragile these animals are.
2. **Don't allow kids** to carry puppies or kittens because these little animals need proper support.
3. **Tell children that** pets need to be talked to in a quiet, kind voice.
4. **Provide a safe place** for your pet, where he or she can go that your young children can't.
5. **Allow all pets** complete quiet and privacy when they're eating. Don't allow your children or any other family member to talk to or approach pets then.
6. **Never allow** any family member to tease a pet or to play aggressive games with it, such as the pet and the human tugging on the opposite ends of towels or socks.

Chapter 10

8-Minute Emergency Cleaning Plan

"Courage is grace under pressure."

—Ernest Hemingway, novelist

It's 5:30 p.m. You just got home from work, where the air-conditioning went on the fritz the last hour. Then:

Surprise! Your life partner's relatives you've never met are dropping by in 15 minutes on their way through town on vacation.

Or:

Your daughter's Girl Scout leader is coming right over for an informal chat.

Or:

The pastor at your church wants to stop by in 20 minutes to "share" with you about your son's behavior in confirmation class.

IMPORTANT: Don't Panic

Chances are if you dropped by these folks' places without much warning, you see tumbleweeds of dust bunnies and old piles of magazines too. You're a good Mom and you love your kids—that's what really matters. And didn't you read somewhere that the average person eats about 60,000 pounds of food during his or her lifetime? (Yes, it's true, according to turnerlearning.com.) So it's logical that, if you have two kids, some of this food could be sitting out at your house.

Here's the 8 Minute Plan

1. Go grab the biggest laundry basket you have.

   Time: **30 seconds**

2. Run through the main rooms only, putting these and similar items in your basket: crumpled newspapers, remotes, magazines, used tissues, hockey gear, the cat's half-chewed feather toy, and naked troll dolls.

   Time: **2 minutes**

3. Shove the basket into a bedroom closet and firmly shut the door.

   Time: **30 seconds**

4. Pick up any kind of air freshener, even the smelly, fake pine tree one if you have to—no time to be picky. Starting in your entryway and spray the stuff liberally in every room, giving the kids' rooms a couple of extra squirts.

Time: **1 minute**

5. Close the doors to the kids' rooms and basement.

Time: **30 seconds**

6. Find a clean rag and some furniture polish. If you can't find a clean rag, a kind-of-clean one will do. Spray polish only on the main living area's coffee table. Polish with the cloth.

Time: **1 minute**

7. Put some nice tunes on your CD or tape player.

   * Select crooners for the 65-plus crowd

   * Choose old time rock 'n' roll for 50s boomers.

   * Pick alternative rock for the under-30 crowd

Time: **1 minute**

8. Dim the lights, leaving just enough on so people won't fall. If you don't have dimmers, turn on minimal lighting. What dirt they can't see can't worry them or you.

Time: **30 seconds**

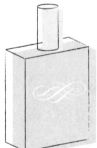

9. Sprinkle a little cologne on yourself if there's some handy.

Time: **1 minute**

WOW—you did it in just 8 minutes!

Use Only in Extreme Emergencies

There's also a 5-minute plan for those guests who only give you 5 minutes notice. There are only three simple steps:

1. **Drag out the vacuum cleaner.** Put it in a prominent corner.
2. **Squirt furniture polish** into the air of the living room.
3. **Put the can of furniture polish** and a clean or semiclean rag in the middle of the coffee table.

When guests arrive, act happy to see them. Then say, "I apologize for my messy house, but I was just getting ready to clean."

Stay-At-Home Moms Would Earn $134,121 Yearly

A full-time stay-at-home mother would earn $134,121 a year if paid for all her work, according to Salary.com, based in Waltham, Massachusetts. The amount is similar to that earned by top U.S. advertising executives, marketing directors, or judges.

A mother who works outside the home would earn an extra $85,876 annually on top of wages for the work she does at home, the study says. This is based on wages of a housekeeper, day care teacher, cook, computer whiz, laundry machine operator, janitor, facilities manager, van driver, chief executive, and psychologist. No wonder Moms are tired!

DID YOU KNOW?

- The year 1954 saw the introduction of color choices in appliances. Today it's a trend that's making a big comeback.
- The first microwave oven was introduced in 1955 and cost $7,000. Isn't it nice to know that the prices on some things have actually gone down?

Memo from mom

PLAY THE 15-MINUTE LIMIT GAME

With six kids and a houseful of typically untidy bedrooms, we've turned cleaning time into "contest time." I get everything ready in the hallway outside the kids' bedrooms. The vacuum is plugged in and ready. The dusting spray, rags, and window cleaner are there.

I blow my whistle, then I promptly set an egg timer for 15 minutes and watch the workers fly. The kids know they have to do the following in just 15 minutes:

1. Pick up dirty clothes and put them in the laundry hamper.

2. Pick up trash and put it in the wastebasket.

3. Make their beds.

4. Pick up their clean clothes, fold them, and put them away again.

5. Pick up toys and put them away.

6. Make sure everything is in its place, including things that don't really belong in their rooms. I'm talking dirty glasses, kitchen plates, scotch tape, and snow shovels (don't ask).

All that is done in 15 short minutes while everyone has fun; the winner gets to pick the evening meal. Now that's a winning plan all the way around.

Anonymous mom from San Diego, California

Chapter 11

Lowdown on Laundry

"Behind every successful woman is a basket of dirty laundry."
—Sally Forth, comic strip heroine

No one thinks it's fun. (If you do, consider starting your own laundry business!) But like taxes, doing laundry is a fact of life.

Busy moms have the unique opportunity to become experienced at this life skill and pass it down to their children. With the hints and tips in this chapter, you'll conquer this task more easily than you'd think.

The first thing to consider is where you want to locate your laundry center. If you're lucky enough to put the laundry center wherever you want it, consider the sites below.

The Basement

This area requires climbing steps while carrying baskets but keeps your living space clear. Spills, splashes, or overflow may do less damage. Include a scrub sink for hand laundry. A drying rack or indoor clothesline is good for drip drying and saving energy.

The Bathroom/Dressing Room

Plumbing is handy—convenient for doing daily laundry. But leaks could damage floors and ceilings if it's on the upper level.

The Bedroom Area

Having a washer and dryer in a utility closet saves steps. But leaks could damage carpets, floors, and ceilings if it's on an upper floor.

The Kitchen

A laundry in or near the kitchen is good for handy plumbing and easy multitasking chores. Cabinets provide storage space for supplies.

Get Prepared

A tidy, well-functioning laundry room will make this regular task seem less of a chore. Here are some ideas to turn your laundry area into an efficient area:

 TIP 509 **Install uniform,** glare-free light so you can easily inspect, sort, and fold laundry.

 TIP 510 **Purchase low-cost shelving** or cabinets to keep supplies handy.

 TIP 511 **Change a closet** into a laundry room with stackable storage units. Install racks for laundry supplies on the back of the closet door.

 TIP 512 **Buy a closet rod** for clothes that you hang directly out of the dryer. Use double rods if you hang primarily shirts and slacks. Add another rack for socks.

 TIP 513 **Use a table** for folding and sorting. It doesn't need to be fancy; even a card table will do.

 TIP 514 **Put an ironing board** and iron in the laundry room.

 TIP 515 **Hang the ironing board** from a heavy-duty storage hook in your laundry room if the room doesn't have a closet.

 TIP 516 **Keep all laundry** products out of children's reach on upper shelves or in locked cabinets.

 TIP 517 **Keep products off** the washer and dryer. Drips could damage exterior surfaces. If you spill wipe the area clean immediately.

Gather Your Supplies

The typical American laundry room contains these products for maximum efficiency. *(If you're interested in cleaning green, see Chapter 7 for alternative products.)*

- Ammonia, nonsudsing
- Antistatic dryer sheets
- Baking soda
- Bleach (all-fabric, color safe)
- Bleach (regular)
- Drying racks
- Enzyme pretreatment stain removers
- Gentle detergent for fine washables
- Heavy-duty laundry detergent
- Ironing board and iron
- Laundry detergent
- Oxygen detergent boosters
- Pretreatment stain removers
- Sponges to wipe up spills
- Spray starch
- White paper towels
- White vinegar

Guide to Treating Common Fabrics

Acrylic knit

Normally this is machine washable. Read the label to check for proper drying procedures. Some knits keep their shape best if dried flat.

Cotton

This fabric is known for holding up well to home laundering. Remove any cotton items from the dryer promptly to reduce wrinkling (and save you time ironing). Iron using spray starch for the crispness of a professionally laundered shirt.

Cotton blend

Dry these items on the permanent-press or low cycle and remove immediately to reduce wrinkling. Touch up with a steam iron; starch for a professional look.

Linen

These items may be dry-cleaned or handwashed. Read care labels. Use a steam iron for a crisp look.

Polyester

Read the label. Normally machine washing (cool water) and drying (low setting) is best. Read the item's label to see if air-drying is recommended. Touch up with a cool iron—never hot—and only do this if necessary.

Silk

Professional cleaning is best. Some silks are hand- or machine-washable. Never machine-dry these.

DID YOU KNOW?
Fun Facts About Laundry

- Americans wash about 35 billion loads of laundry a year.
- The typical load of laundry is 10 pounds.
- The average family in the United States spends $10 monthly on laundry detergent.
- The average American household does 400 loads of laundry a year.

Wool knit

Wool can be dry-cleaned, but check the label. If the label says the item is hand-washable, use cool water and gentle detergent. Rinse well and lay flat to retain the item's original shape.

Avoid Laundry Mishaps

If you have doubts about the colorfastness of an item, wash it separately in a low-water setting or a minibasket if your machine has one. Or mix a small amount of detergent with a cup of warm water. Moisten an inner seam or inconspicuous spot. Rub the spot with a clean, dry, white towel. If the color comes off, launder the garment separately. Here are some other ways to steer clear of laundry problems:

 Check pockets for pens, crayons, coins, and tissues. Tissues can be a real mess to pick off everything. (A good way to teach kids about this is to have them help you pick off tissue residue.) Pens, crayons, and coins can cause your washing machine to break down.

 Look for crayons in pockets. If they survive the wash, they melt in the dryer, staining clothing.

 Pretreat soiled shirt collars and cuffs with a prewash stain removal product or liquid laundry detergent.

 Use pretreatment gels and sticks on protein stains such as grass and baby formula. Apply them directly to the stain. But don't use pretreatment gels or sticks on light or fluorescent colors.

 Measure out the recommended amount of detergent. Too much means extra rinsing; too little may not clean well.

TIP 523 **Dissolve detergent** in warm water first. If your washing machine has it, use an automatic water-temperature control for maximum efficiency.

 TIP 524 **Turn fine washables** inside out and use the delicate or knit setting if you machine-wash them.

 TIP 525 **Inspect clothes** for stains before both washing and drying. If a stain remains after laundering, treat it with a stain removal product and rewash.

 TIP 526 **Blot, don't rub,** a fresh stain before pretreating or laundering it. Blotting draws the stain away from fabric; rubbing pushes it into the fabric.

 TIP 527 **Use light-colored** terry cloth towels or cloths when blotting stains—lint and dye could transfer from dark colors and may make things worse.

 TIP 528 **Maximize towel absorbency** by adding a cup of white vinegar to the rinse water once a month. Dry as usual. (Vinegar is good for removing excess detergent.)

 TIP 529 **Wash heavily stained** items separately to avoid transferring stains.

TIP 530 **Skip hot water** on stains of unknown origin. It sets protein stains.

Washing Machines

 Keep your washing machine clean. Wipe out the soap, bleach, or fabric softener compartments regularly. For front-loading machines, wipe the rubber door gasket where the water often collects in the fold.

 Check washer hoses periodically by turning the water on and feeling for bulges. Replace hoses that have bulges.

 Never overload your washer. It leaves less room for water, limiting the effective cleaning and damaging fabrics. "Walking" machines that shift out of position and go noisily off balance during spin cycles are a result of overloading.

HOW TO READ CARE LABELS

Hot water: Water up to 150°F

Warm water: Water between 90° and 110° degrees F

Cold water: Water up to 85°F

Durable or permanent-press cycle: Cool rinse before spinning (reduces wrinkling)

With like colors: Wash with clothing of similar brightness and color

Dry flat: Lay out horizontally to dry

Block to dry: Reshape to original dimensions

No chlorine bleach: Chlorine bleach may harm the item

Add liquid fabric softeners to the final rinse water in the washing machine. Fabric softeners make ironing easier. They also prevent static electricity from forming on manufactured fibers.

 Make sure your washer and dryer are installed properly and your dryer is vented correctly for maximum efficiency. You'll save on your energy bill if you do.

 Have your washer and dryer checked by a professional at least yearly. This will keep them operating at peak efficiency, another way to save on your energy costs.

 Use nonabrasive cleaners on the outside of your washing and drying machines. Abrasive cleaners may scratch the surfaces.

Dryer Care

 Clean the lint trap on the dryer before each load. A full lint trap reduces efficiency and is a fire hazard.

 Check dryer doors for tightness by moving a piece of tissue paper around the door's edge while the dryer is on. Have the seal checked regularly.

 Clean the dryer lint screen at least every six months with a nylon brush, as follows:
1. Wet both sides of the lint screen with hot water.
2. Wet the nylon brush with hot water and liquid detergent; scrub the lint screen with the brush to remove residue buildup.
3. Rinse the screen, dry it, and replace it.

The Busy Moms' Guide to Getting Out Stains

Alcoholic beverages

Wash the item with detergent in water as hot as is safe for the fabric.

Baby formula

Pretreat or soak stains with a product containing enzymes. Soak for at least 30 minutes. Launder normally. (Always launder infants' clothing in mild detergent for baby clothes.)

Baby spit-ups

Apply a liberal amount of water to set stains. Then sprinkle powdered dishwasher detergent on them and let the item set for at least 12 hours. Launder as usual.

Ball point pen

Spray or dab the stains with dry-cleaning solvent. Then rub them with heavy-duty liquid detergent. Wash the item with detergent and all-fabric bleach.

Beer

Wash the item with laundry detergent in water as hot as is safe for the fabric.

Bird droppings

For fresh stains use a pretreatment before laundering. If the stain has aged or remains after laundering soak the stained area for about an hour in an enzyme-base laundry booster.

Blood

For fresh stains soak in cold water (hot water will set this stain). Then launder with detergent and an oxygen booster. For dried stains, pretreat or soak in warm water with an enzyme product; launder. If the stain remains, use a bleach safe for the fabric.

Blueberry

Pretreat the stain with heavy-duty liquid laundry detergent. Rinse. Soak fabric in a diluted solution of all-fabric powdered bleach and water. Don't dry in the dryer. The heat will set in any remaining stain.

Breast milk

Pretreat the item with an enzyme product and then launder as usual.

Butter

Pretreat with a prewash stain remover or liquid laundry detergent. Wash using the hottest water safe for the fabric.

Chocolate

Pretreat stains with an enzyme product or prewash stain remover; launder. If the stain remains, rewash with bleach safe for the fabric.

Clay

Remove any remaining clay with a soft scraping tool such as a spoon. Soak the stain in clear water for about 20 minutes before pretreating the stain and laundering as usual.

Coffee or tea

Pretreat these stains with stain remover or liquid laundry detergent. Or rub them with bar soap. Then launder them as usual. Rewash them if needed.

Collar and cuff soil

Pretreat with a general laundry stain remover, liquid laundry detergent, or a paste of detergent and water.

Cooking fats and oils

Wash the item in heavy-duty detergent and hot water. For difficult stains, use a pretreatment product on the stain before washing the item.

Cough syrup

Soak the item 15-30 minutes in 1 quart of warm water, $\frac{1}{2}$ teaspoon liquid dishwashing detergent, and 1 tablespoon white vinegar. Rinse thoroughly. Launder as usual.

Crayon

For a few spots, scrape off excess with a dull knife. Place stained area between white paper towels and press with a warm iron. Reposition paper towels as the crayon is absorbed. To remove stain, place spot facedown on several layers of white paper towels. Sponge the back with a prewash stain remover and then blot with white paper towels

Crayon (continued)

Dry naturally before laundering with detergent and chlorine or colorsafe bleach.

For an entire load affected by crayons, pretreat or soak in a product containing enzymes or chlorine or color safe bleach. Using the hottest water safe for the fabric, rewash with detergent and 1 cup baking soda.

Cream

Rinse the item in cold water and wash with detergent.

Crude oil or tar

Treat stains with a petroleum-base solvent pretreatment spray. Then wash the item with heavy-duty detergent and hot water.

Deodorant

Apply heavy-duty liquid detergent directly on the stains. Wash the item in detergent and warm water.

(Note: A buildup of aluminum from deodorant may be permanent.)

Diaper rash cream

Scrape away remaining cream with a soft scraping tool such as a spoon. Use a pretreatment prior to laundering as usual. Don't dry. Check the item again and repeat the laundering process if any stain remains.

Diesel fuel or gasoline

Use extra caution—these stains make clothing flammable. Use only detergent-base stain removers, not solvent-base ones. Air items thoroughly. Don't place in the dryer if there's a fuel smell.

Dyes

Marks caused by dyes may be difficult to remove. Rinse the area with cold water and treat it with liquid detergent. If the stain persists, soak the item in a diluted solution of powdered all-fabric bleach. Then wash it in detergent and bleach.

Egg

Soak the stains in cold water and launder as usual

Memo from mom

THREE'S A CHARM

Here are three little tips that save me time and energy each week. I hope you can put them to good use.

1. I bought four dishpans, a different color for each member of the family, and placed them on a shelf near the washing machine. I fold directly into the pans so that they're sorted and packaged for each person. Theoretically the kids are supposed to put their clothes away when I announce, "The laundry is finished." Actually, they pretty much live out of the dishpans until the next week. But at least things stay neat, and they can find what they want.

2. If for some reason you don't have a cordless phone, get one! There's always something you can do while talking, and a cordless phone frees you to do it.

3. I made an aisle-by-aisle list of the grocery stores I use most frequently and keep it in the computer to print out as needed. I transfer my fridge list to the floor-plan list, add items from my weekly menu (planned in advance), and go. Working this way tells you what you need when you get to every aisle. It's incredibly efficient and saves at least 20 minutes each time I go to the store.

—from Del Perkins, Mobile, Alabama
A busy mom to Hank, 16 years old, and Aline, 14 years old

Feces

Scrape off any solid matter. Soak the item in cold water and launder as usual.

Felt-tip pen

Pretreat the area with heavy-duty liquid detergent and rinse well. If the stain persists, soak the item in a diluted solution of all-fabric bleach. Then wash it in detergent and bleach safe for the fabric.

Fruit and fruit juices

Mix $\frac{1}{2}$ cup cool water, $\frac{1}{4}$ cup baking soda, and 1 tablespoon borax. Apply the solution to stains and let the item set for 20 minutes. Rinse in cool water and launder as usual.

Furniture polish

Rub heavy-duty liquid detergent into the stained area and launder as usual.

Grass

Pretreat the item with a stain remover or liquid laundry detergent. Launder using the hottest water safe for the fabric. For heavy stains, place items facedown on several layers of white paper towels. Apply the cleaning fluid to the back of the stain. Replace towels as the stain is absorbed. Let dry; rinse and launder.

Gravy

Pretreat or soak with a product containing enzymes. Soak for 30 minutes if the stain is dry. Launder as usual.

Grease

Treat stains with a petroleum-base solvent pretreatment spray. Then wash the item with heavy-duty detergent in hot water.

Hair dye

Loosen the stain with hairspray. Launder as usual.

Hair spray

Rub stains with heavy-duty laundry detergent. Then wash the item, using detergent and all-fabric bleach. If the fabric is colorfast, you can wash it with chlorine bleach.

DID YOU KNOW?

Kids and Laundry

It may not surprise you that households with children use more laundry detergent than those without. Households with kids aged 6 to 17 buy more than their expected share of heavy-duty liquid detergents, according to the Neilsen report.

Hobby glue

Scrape away any remaining glue with a soft scraping tool such as a spoon. Soak the garment (30 minutes for fresh stains, several hours for set-in stains) in cold water and rinse. Check the garment. If the stain remains, soak another 30 minutes. Rewash. Repeat until the stain has disappeared. Follow the garment label warnings and the manufacturer's instructions.

Ice cream

Soak stains in cold water. Launder as usual.

Ink (permanent)

Pretreat stains with heavy-duty liquid detergent and rinse well. If stains persist, soak the item in a diluted solution of powdered all-fabric bleach. Wash it in detergent and bleach that are safe for the fabric.

Ink (washable)

Wash with detergent. Don't use bleach.

Iodine

Treat stains with sodium thiosulfate (available in photo supply stores as "acid fixer"). If the solution contains other chemicals, don't use it.

Jam

Soak the item in cold water. Launder as usual.

Ketchup

Rub the stains with waterless hand cleaner and rinse the item in cold water. Launder as usual.

Lipstick

Sponge or soak using cool water; pretreat. Launder with bleach.

Liquid paper

Blot excess fluid and allow the item to dry completely. Brush away dried particles. Use a pretreatment stain remover. Rinse. Rub liquid detergent into the stain, soak, and launder as usual.

Makeup

Rub stains with heavy-duty liquid detergent. Then wash the item, using detergent and all-fabric bleach. If the fabric is colorfast, you can use chlorine bleach instead of all-fabric bleach.

Mayonnaise

Scrape off the excess with a dull knife. Wash the item in heavy-duty detergent using water as hot as is safe for the fabric.

Meat juice

Soak in cold water. Launder as usual.

Mildew

Brush the item outdoors so mildew won't spread inside the house. Pretreat the affected area with heavy-duty liquid detergent and bleach. Wash the item in hot water with heavy-duty detergent safe for the fabric.

Milk

Soak the item in cold water. Launder as usual.

Mud/dirt

Allow the mud to dry. Brush off as much as possible before washing. For really tough stains, use a pretreatment product, then soak in laundry detergent for at least 30 minutes; launder.

Mustard

Pretreat with stain remover. Launder with bleach.

Nail polish

Place the stain facedown on layers of white paper towels. Apply polish remover to the back of the stain. Replace the towels as they accept the polish. Repeat, rinse, and launder.

Nicotine

Blot the stain with eucalyptus oil (available in health-food stores) and launder as usual.

Olive oil

Pretreat with a prewash stain remover or liquid laundry detergent. Wash using the hottest water safe for the fabric.

Orange juice (fresh)

Fresh orange juice spills can usually be removed by washing in detergent and hot water. Old stains may need to be bleached for removal.

Paint (oil-base)

If the paint label recommends a thinner, use that solvent for stain removal. Or sponge with turpentine; rinse. Pretreat with a prewash stain remover, bar soap, or laundry detergent. Rinse, launder, or take to a dry cleaner.

Paint (water-base)

Rinse the fabric in warm water while the stains are wet; launder. For dried paint, take the item to a dry cleaner.

Peanut butter

Scrape away any excess peanut butter with a spoon. Spray the area with a pretreatment gel or spray. Rub liquid laundry detergent on the area and let it set for a few minutes. Launder as usual.

Perfume

Don't use bath soap or dishwashing liquid. Wash the item in detergent.

Perspiration

Apply liquid detergent directly to the stain. Or presoak the garment for 15 to 30 minutes in liquid detergent and water. Launder using the hottest water safe for the fabric.

Pesticides

Never wash pesticide-soiled items with other laundry.

Petroleum lip balm

Pretreat with a concentrated grease removal product. Launder as usual.

ABCs OF WASHERS AND DRYERS

Washers and dryers are 24 to 33 inches wide. Front-loading washers are more accessible to wheelchair users.

Stacked units use less than 33 inches of floor space and fit in small spaces. They're perfect for small apartments or townhouses with limited square footage.

Wash basket dimensions

Size	Cubic Feet (cf)
Compact	1.7-2.3 cf
Medium	2.1-2.5 cf
Large	2.7-3 cf
Extra Large	3.1 or more cf

Dryer drum dimensions

Size	Cubic Feet (cf)
Compact	2-4 cf
Medium	4-5.8 cf
Large	5.9-6.9 cf
Extra Large	7 or more cf

Washer options

- Heavy-duty, presoak, and prewash cycles
- Digital displays
- High-efficiency units that save water and energy
- Delay-start features
- Indicates time remaining left in the cycle
- Automatic water-level controls
- Stainless-steel or polypropylene tubs (smooth and rustproof)
- Spin cycles of 700 to 1,600 revolutions per minute, spinning loads nearly dry

Dryer options

- High efficiency units that save water and energy
- Lower heat, super-delicate setting
- Indicates time remaining left to dry
- Durable glass doors, so you can see inside
- Easy-to-read LCD displays
- Drying sensors that help the machine not overdry
- Automatic lock that keeps children from opening the door
- A drying rack

Red wine

Sponge or soak the stain, using cool water. Pretreat with a stain remover or liquid laundry detergent. Launder with bleach.

Rust

Don't use chlorine bleach; it sets the stain. Treat the affected area with a commercial rust remover.

Salad dressing

Scrape the excess off with a dull knife. Wash the item in heavy-duty detergent, using water as hot as is safe for the fabric.

Salt

Remove salt marks from shoes and leather garments by wiping them with a solution of 1 part vinegar and 3 parts water.

Scorch marks

Launder using chlorine bleach, if it's safe for the fabric. Otherwise soak the item in color-safe bleach and the hottest water safe for the fabric; launder.

Self-tanning lotion

Dab the stain with hydrogen peroxide and then launder as usual.

Shoe polish

Spray or dab the stains with dry-cleaning solvent. Then rub them with heavy-duty liquid detergent and launder as usual.

Smoke damage

Shake off soot outdoors. Launder using a heavy-duty phosphate-base detergent or heavy-duty liquid detergent. Add 1 cup water conditioner and $\frac{1}{2}$ cup all-fabric bleach to the wash cycle. Use the water setting recommended for the fabric. Allow to air-dry. Inspect the garment and repeat if necessary.

Soft drinks

Launder as usual. Don't use bar soap to try to remove the stain.

Soy sauce

If possible don't let the stain dry. Blot the stain with a towel. Use a pretreatment and launder in cool water. If stains remain use an enzyme product to help break down the sauce and relaunder. For aged, set-in stains, apply a glycerin solution and let set for 25 minutes. Then treat as previously recommended.

Steak sauce

Saturate stain with laundry pretreatment (aerosol types work best for this kind of stain). Wait 3 minutes. Launder immediately. If stain remains soak in chlorine bleach or in oxygen bleach, whichever is safest for the fabric.

Tempura paint

Pretreat the stain with a heavy-duty liquid detergent and rinse thoroughly. If the stain is on white or colorfast material, soak the garment in a diluted powdered bleach and water mixture for about 15 minutes.

Tomato sauce

Apply prewash stain remover or liquid laundry detergent. Wash with liquid laundry detergent, using bleach and water temperature safe for the fabric.

Urine, vomit, mucus

Soak the stains in cold water. Launder using chlorine bleach (which disinfects), colorsafe bleach, or oxygen booster.

Vegetable oil

Treat the stain with a petroleum-base solvent pretreatment spray. Wash the item with heavy-duty detergent in hot water.

Water spots

Launder garments as usual. For dry-cleanable fabrics, consult a professional dry cleaner.

Wax

Use a dull knife to scrape off as much as possible. For remaining wax, place between paper towels and press with a warm iron. Replace towels as the wax is absorbed. Launder as usual.

Solve Common Laundry Problems

Blue stains

Detergent or fabric softener may not be dissolving. If detergent causes the problem, soak the garment in a plastic container using 1 cup white vinegar to 1 quart water. Soak for one hour; rinse and launder. To avoid these stains, add the detergent and turn on warm water before adding laundry. If using fabric softener, rub stains with bar soap. Rinse and launder.

Detergent powder residue

Causes include undissolved detergent or low water temperature. Add detergent and dissolve it in warm water before adding laundry.

Grayness (overall)

This could be caused by low water temperature, incorrect sorting (resulting in dirt or color transfer), or not enough detergent. To solve this problem, increase the wash cycle temperature. Sort heavily soiled from lightly soiled items and carefully sort by color. Use the right amount of detergent with bleach.

Grayness (uneven)

Usually this is caused by not using enough detergent. Rewash with the correct amount and the hottest water safe for the fabric.

Lint

This can be caused by mixing items such as bath towels and napped velour or corduroy, a clogged washer lint filter, a full dryer lint screen, or tissues left in the pockets of garments. Rewash separately.

Pilling

This is a wear problem of some synthetic and permanent-press fabrics. Use a lint brush or roller with masking tape to remove pills. Adding a fabric softener may help.

Shrinkage

This is irreversible damage. Avoid shrinkage by following labels' instructions. Wash items in warm water and rinse in cold. Reduce drying time and remove garments when slightly damp.

Stiffness or fading

Hard water may cause stiffness and fading. Use liquid detergent or add a water softener product.

Worn areas

Prevent worn areas by placing delicate items, such as fine lingerie or hose, in mesh bags made for washing delicates. This helps to avoid abrasion from other garments or the washer agitator.

Yellowing

Buildup of body soil may cause yellowing. Use a detergent booster or bleach safe for the fabric type.

Handling Special Laundering

Antique linens

Very old lace or fabrics may tear if washed. Linens at antiques fairs usually are already cleaned and pressed, but if you find fabrics at a garage sale or antiques shop, you'll want to clean them.

Bedding

Wash sheets in warm water, using nonchlorine bleach when needed. Wash all-cotton spreads, blankets, and coverlets in cold water. Naturally refresh pillows, comforters, and duvets by airing them outside on a sunny day.

DID YOU KNOW?
Overtime Is Killing Us!

As very tired Moms/psychologists/janitors know, their work is far more than a full-time job, and overtime is the killer. The average **stay-at-home Mom works almost 92 hours per week.**

Employed mothers reported spending on average 44 hours per week at their outside job and then another 49.8 hours at their home job. Nice to know that Moms earn their collective exhaustion.

Chenille

Wash these items in the washing machine on the delicate setting and dry them in the dryer on the low setting. If you need to iron them, lay the fabric, tufted side down, on a well-padded ironing board and use the cotton setting.

Children's sleepwear

Never use chlorine bleach on flame-resistant fabrics. It reduces the effectiveness of the treatment chemicals and might ruin treated fabrics. Follow the care instructions on the label.

Comforters

Even in large dryers, only twin comforters can fit. You'll need to take larger comforters to the dry cleaners.

Electric blankets

These can be gently laundered to extend blanket life and keep them fresh. Here's how:

- Disconnect the electrical cord.

- Check the care label.

- Pretreat soiled areas.

- Fill the washer with warm water to the highest level.

- Add liquid laundry detergent; agitate briefly.

- Set the washer for 2 minutes of gentle agitation; start the washer.

- Put three or four clean, dry bath towels into the dryer.

- Load the blanket into the dryer with warm towels.

- Set the timed drying cycle for 20 minutes; start the dryer.

- Check the blanket after it's in the dryer 10 minutes. Continue drying only if the blanket is sopping wet.

- Remove the slightly damp blanket (over drying damages wiring and causes shrinkage).

Electric blankets (continued)

- Hang the blanket over two lines or lay flat until dry.

- If the blanket has scorching, loose connections, or damaged, worn cords or wiring, discard the blanket.

Embroidered items

Test the embroidery for colorfastness by gently dabbing the thread on the back of the piece with a damp white cloth. If no color comes off on the cloth, you can hand wash the piece safely. Press while damp.

Lacy, fringed items

To clean pieces with handmade lace, fringe, or crocheted edging, presoak them for 5 minutes in clear water. Gently swish linens in warm water with mild detergent. Don't use bleach because it can cause damage.

Quilts (vintage)

Launder as little as possible. Check with quilting or fabric shops for products formulated especially for washing quilts. Quits can be professionally dry-cleaned by a laundry that specializes in fine linens

Hand Laundry How-Tos

 Use a mild laundry detergent or product.

 Fill a sink or small tub with water and detergent. Soak the garment; never scrub or twist. Rinse with clear water.

 Gently squeeze out excess water. Don't wring.

 Roll heavy garments in white cotton terry towels to remove excess water.

Tips on Folding

 Casual shirts or T-shirts—hold the shirt by the shoulder seams near the neck seam, with the front facing you. Fold the sleeves and sides back so the sleeves meet in the middle of the back. Drape the sleeves flat along folded edges. Fold the garment from top to bottom. It's easy to show your kids how to do this.

 Slacks—line up the seams and the hems when folding slacks to help keep creases crisp.

 Fitted sheets—fold in half lengthwise and again top to bottom, smoothing out wrinkles. Fold into thirds.

 Flat sheets—fold with the right side out. Fold the bottom to the top, smooth them, and then fold them top to bottom again. Next, fold them side to side, aligning the hems.

 Rectangular tablecloths—fold as you would a flat sheet.

 Round tablecloths—fold in half, wrong sides together, to make a half circle. Fold it in half again.

 Towels—fold to half their width, then fold into thirds. This way they'll be ready to hang on the towel bars. Even little kids can help you with this.

Most Dangerous Cleaning Products for Kids

Many products, including very strong chemicals, are in our homes and often within reach of children (or pets). Unfortunately, leaving cleaning products within reach leads to poisoned children. They may swallow, inhale, or get cleaning products into their eyes or on their skin. Here are some of the most dangerous products for children:

- **Combinations of products.** A mixture of bleach and ammonia produces a very irritating gas called chloramine. A mixture of bleach and an acid such as a toilet bowl cleaner produces chlorine gas, which is even more dangerous. Both can damage lungs and cause breathing problems.

- **Oven cleaners,** drain openers, and toilet bowl cleaners. These products burn every body area that they touch. While swallowing them is certainly dangerous, they also can cause skin burns and eye burns if there is any contact.

- **Polishes and waxes.** When children swallow these products, they may gag, cough, and choke. That allows the material to go down into their lungs. This can cause lung irritation and pneumonia.

- **Rust removers.** Many contain a chemical called hydroflupuoric acid. In a low concentration, this doesn't cause surface burns. But if it is absorbed through skin, it can cause severe pain and heart problems.

Use These Precautions

Commercial cleaning products can keep homes tidy and attractive. When you use them, follow these precautions:

- **Consider doing heavy-duty cleaning** when children (and pets) are not around. This decreases the chances for poison exposure and decreases other dangers too—for example, falling into a bucket of water on a slippery floor.

- **Do not mix** cleaning products unless the label specifically says it's all right.

- **Follow safety precautions** on the label. Common examples are letting plenty of fresh air into the room or wearing rubber gloves.

- **Read and follow** label directions for safe use.

- **Replace** child-resistant caps after use.

- **Store products** in their original containers. Serious poisonings can occur when cleaners are transferred to food or soda containers and left out.

ASK THE EXPERTS

If you suspect your child has been poisoned, call the **National Capital Poison Center at 800-222-1222.**

Chapter 12

Those Other Rooms

"My second favorite household chore is ironing. My first is hitting my head on top of the bunkbed until I faint."

—Erma Bombeck, author

Attics, basements, and garages pose special cleaning challenges. They get dirtier than the rest of the house, yet they're usually cleaned less often. So dirt and dust buildup can be tough to clean.

These spots also require organization before you get to the actual cleaning. In this chapter you'll find the best ways to:

- Clean concrete walls and floors
- Keep stored items dry and mildew free
- Maintain windows and floors
- Protect these areas from insects
- Store items using proper containers

 Don't use cardboard boxes to store items. They can absorb moisture from concrete walls and floors. Mildew may form on the boxes and items inside.

 Use charcoal in net vegetable bags to get rid of stale, musty odors. Use the kind that onions come in and hang one in each corner.

 Remove mold and mildew odors by placing 1 cup white vinegar in opposite corners of a room (on the floor, under a table, or behind a piece of furniture) for 24 hours.

TIP 555 **Avoid mothballs.** They contain naphthalene, a poison when it's inhaled or eaten. Symptoms include headache, nausea, vomiting, shortness of breath, coughing, and burning eyes.

Get Rid of Four-Legged Pests

 Prevent termites in attics, basements, and garages with these strategies:

1. Repair leaky irrigation valves, spigots, or watering lines.
2. Don't keep firewood in the garage.
3. Remove leaves near your home.
4. Support fence posts and porch pillars with concrete footing. Placing fence posts directly in the ground can attract termites.
5. Make sure water drains away from your house.
6. Call a professional termite remover if you suspect your home is infested.

 Avoid crickets by storing boxes off floors and keeping them tightly sealed. Fix leaks around the house. Seal openings into your home where crickets can live and mate.

 Stall scorpions by removing lumber, trash, old boxes and old clothes. Remove clutter from basements, attics and garages so scorpions don't have a place to hide. Check cracks, crevices, and the foundation to stop their entry into your home.

Attack That Attic

The best thing about cleaning the attic is that all you need to tackle it are some old jeans and a T-shirt to wear. A few hours a day will allow you to go through the boxes at a leisurely pace. Or block out 3 to 4 hours on the weekend to get it done all at once. If you can get your kids to help, it might only take two hours.

Dust starting high and slowly work your way down. Clean cobwebs out before you dust, working from the bottom up.

 Prevent dampness and mold by cleaning filters on humidifiers, dehumidifiers, air purifiers, and air conditioners regularly. Ventilate the attic as often as possible to keep storage items dry and free from musty smells.

 Don't vacuum or sweep the attic (or any other area) if you think rodents might be there. Some diseases carried by rodents are commonly contracted by breathing airborne particles. Call a professional pest control expert.

 Use a dust mop or broom covered with a cloth to dust the rafters, ceiling, walls, and floors. Change or shake the cloth frequently.

 Dust attic floors with a cloth-covered broom. Follow with a wet cleaning of clear water on wood floors. Wipe them dry fast.

 Keep humidity levels below 50 percent to prevent water condensation, which can breed bacteria.

 Mark boxes with the date you go through them when you clean, plus a list of the contents. Then check them again in another year. If you haven't used anything from the box in a year, consider donating the contents to a local charity.

 Beware of black mold. Signs are a musty odor from the walls or floor or discolored walls. Black mold (stachybotrys) can cause allergies, sinusitis, asthma, infections, and eczema.

Selling your home? Cleaning your attic is crucial. Buyers always look in the attic to check out the space. Make sure there's adequate lighting, paint the walls and floors if needed, and organize and stack boxes neatly.

 Store luggage in the attic. This way pieces will be clean for their next use. Put a fresh dryer sheet in each piece of luggage to keep interiors smelling clean. Or fill them with neatly folded, out-of-season clothes.

 Organize holiday decorations by dividing them first into groups: lights, ornaments, wreaths, linens, etc.

DID YOU KNOW?
The Best Way to Keep Basements Dry

1. **Grade the foundation** *so that it slopes away from the house. The yard should be graded to direct water toward a drainage area.*

2. **Clear gutters** *of obstructions to direct water away from the house through the downspouts.*

3. **Caulk around** *basement windows and doors.*

4. **Use waterproof paint** *on basement walls to help keep everything mold and mildew free.*

5. **Install a dehumidifier** *in the basement to keep humidity levels between 30 and 50 percent.*

6. **Invest in a sump pump** *with an automatic switch to keep water from backing up.*

7. **Get a water sensor.** *It's an inexpensive backup for your sump pump. It will let you know if the basement surface gets wet.*

BEAT THE CLOCK

1. Store items in see-through tubs, marking the contents and date stored. You'll save time and frustration digging around in boxes to find out what's inside.

2. Sharpen lawn mower blades professionally yearly. This will save you time and energy because sharp blades cut much more quickly and efficiently.

3. Avoid stacking boxes or tubs on top of each other because you'll have to remove the top ones to reach the bottom ones.

4. Put away seasonal lights without tangling them. Cut out a square of cardboard or poster board. Then cut an opening in one side of the square and thread the lights through it. Keep wrapping the string of lights around the piece of cardboard through the opening.

5. Use kitty litter or sawdust to soak up spills in the garage. Sprinkle the litter or sawdust on the spill and allow it to soak up the moisture. Then sweep up the litter and dispose of it.

Battle Basement Blues

The basement sometimes becomes the dumping ground for stuff you can't think where to put anywhere else. Grandma's silver tea set, broken building blocks, or crumbling photos all may fall into that category. Here are some great dos and don'ts for your basement:

 TIP 570 **Use folding screens** to hide stacked boxes in the corner of your basement.

Don't store furniture or electronics in the basement, because of potential dampness. If you must store these items there, get a dehumidifier to take the moisture out of the air. Put the items on pallets so they aren't directly on the floor.

 Check for moisture in the basement. Tape a 1-foot-square piece of aluminum foil to the wall with duct tape. After a few days, check the foil for moisture on both sides. If there is moisture on the side facing the wall, use a masonry sealer to waterproof the wall. If the foil side facing the room is wet, use a dehumidifier.

 Take care of water damage right away. To remove mildew or clean basement floors after water damage, add 4 ounces sodium carbonate to 1 gallon hot water. Scrub the surface, let it sit for 30 minutes, and then rinse with clear water.

 Clean window wells seasonally and caulk around them if needed. This keeps water from building up and seeping in.

 Store paints and other flammable liquids away from the hot water heater and furnace. This will prevent potentially hazardous fires.

 Never store books in your basement. Moisture and mildew may damage pages and expensive leather bindings.

 Keep bulk storage items in airtight containers near the entrance of the basement so that they'll be dry and easily accessible.

 Consider area rugs instead of carpeting for your basement. Unlike carpeting, area rugs can be removed for washing, repair, or replacement.

Remove odors that have seeped into the concrete basement floor with an enzyme cleaner. Let it sit 20 minutes, then rinse well. Vacuum the floor with a wet vacuum. Allow it to dry. If the odor remains, repeat the process. Once the odor is gone, seal the concrete floor.

Organize the Garage

This area can get pretty dirty due to outside elements, yard maintenance equipment, bikes, and cars. Spruce up your garage annually to keep dirt and oil from coming into the house. Here are some great tips:

 Clean unpainted concrete with a mixture of 4 to 6 tablespoons of powdered laundry detergent in 1 gallon of hot water. Then you'll need to seal the surface.

 Store long-handled tools handle side up in an old golf bag or in a large garbage can with wheels. That way you can wheel them around the yard as you're working and see the tool you need without removing several items.

 Keep tools clean and rust free by sticking them into a bucket of sand to store them when not in use.

 Use a loft in the garage for overhead storage space. It's ideal for sports gear and holiday ornaments.

 Get a locking chest or cabinet for dangerous tools and pesticides so the kids and pets can't access them.

 Mount bicycles on the wall. Bicycle shops and home centers have racks for keeping bikes flush to the wall. Add an accessory rack for helmets and equipment.

Wash garage windows with a mixture of 3 tablespoons rubbing alcohol or vinegar, 1 tablespoon household ammonia, and 1 quart warm water.

 Clean lawn mower blades before you mow by spraying them with nonstick cooking spray. The blades will be easier to clean and won't bring shards of grass into the garage.

 Drain gas and oil from your lawn mower at season's end. Put it in a container, mark it clearly, and arrange for hazardous waste disposal. Keep it away from kids and pets.

 Buy only enough pesticides for the current season. Better yet, check gardening books and your county extension service for organic, nonharmful alternatives.

 Hang tools on a pegboard to keep them organized and close at hand.

 Store seasonal small appliances on shelves clearly marked so they're easily accessible.

DID YOU KNOW?
The Best Way to Organize Attic Space

1. *Use the One Year Rule. Mark one container "one year." Fill it with contents you're not sure you want to give up. Then mark the date on the box and check it again in a year. By then you may want to move those contents to "trash" or "donations" boxes.*

2. *Clean, then store. Dry-clean clothes before putting them away. Don't store clothes in dry-cleaning bags because these bags may cause discoloration of the clothes.*

Index